FASTER

FASTER

DEMYSTIFYING THE SCIENCE OF TRIATHLON SPEED

JIM GOURLEY

VELO press

Boulder, Colorado

3002 Sterling Circle, Suite 100
Boulder, Colorado 80301-2338 USA
(303) 440-0601 · Fax (303) 444-6788 · E-mail velopress@competitorgroup.com

Distributed in the United States and Canada by Ingram Publisher Services

Library of Congress Cataloging-in-Publication Data
Gourley, Jim.
  Faster: demystifying the science of triathlon speed / Jim Gourley.
    pages cm
  Includes bibliographical references and index.
  ISBN 978-1-937715-02-1 (pbk. : alk. paper)
1. Triathlon—Training. 2. Running speed. I. Title.
  GV1060.73.G68 2013
  796.42'57071—dc23
                              2013015748

For information on purchasing VeloPress books, please call
(800) 811-4210, ext. 2138, or visit www.velopress.com.

This paper meets the requirements of ANSI/NISO Z39.48-1992 (Permanence of Paper).

Cover and interior design by Kevin Roberson
Cover photograph by Brad Hines
Interior graphics by Killer Infographics
Art direction and interior composition by Vicki Hopewell
Additional composition by Jessica Xavier, Planet X Design

Text set in Scala

13 14 15 / 10 9 8 7 6 5 4 3 2 1

CONTENTS

CHAPTER 1   PHYSICS & THE TRIATHLETE 01

CHAPTER 2   THE SWIM 17

FOREWORD

As the iconic II-time Ironman® champion Lisa Bentley said to me after my very first half-Ironman, "It never gets any easier; you just go faster." This book will not make triathlon training or racing easier, but it will make you smarter. Jim Gourley will tell you that a smarter triathlete is a better triathlete, and I believe he's right. You can use your smarts to get more out of your time and more out of your money. If you want to go faster, this book can help you do that. If you want to go just as fast but spend less money or less time, it can help you do that. Armed with the tools and information you need, you will be able to make the decisions that are right for you.

Faster will help you use the greatest asset you have available to you as an endurance athlete: your brain. Although it's your body that has to get the job done on race day, the decisions you make about training, equipment, and pacing are what really make the difference. Gurus and coaches use a popular adage: You don't need to train harder, you just need to train smarter. If we change the way we think about training, our decisions can be guided by knowledge rather than ego, or whatever it is that makes us lust for carbon fiber.

Triathlon is a hard sport, but it's not a difficult sport. Unlike a technical sport such as pole vaulting, there's nothing so tricky about swimming, biking, or running that a reasonably smart person couldn't figure out if given enough time and money. Jim will tell you that the information in this book isn't rocket science. That said, I suppose with enough time and money and brave monkeys, a lot of triathletes could probably find the drive to figure out rocket science too. Triathletes are not, in my experience, afraid of a challenge. And that's one of the things that makes triathlon so special. But why not save yourself time and money, and read this book instead, especially when the information is put together in such a nice, easy-to-read, and witty package?

If you're a bit skeptical about a nice, easy-to-read, and witty package, that's understandable. Marketing departments specialize in such things, and this book will wise you up to those glossy, want-inspiring advertisements found in print and online media, in your race bags, and pretty much anywhere else marketing departments can put them. Interestingly enough, the word *advertise* comes from the Latin word *advertere*, which means "to turn toward." That's what an advertisement tries to do: turn you toward the product. Now, that doesn't mean that advertisements are inherently misleading. It just means that they have an agenda.

Faster has an agenda too: to make you an informed triathlete. The word *science* derives from the Latin root verb *scire*, meaning "to know." The scientific method is based on developing a theory (or hypothesis) about something, and then coming up with a test (or experiment) to see if you're right . . . or if you're wrong. That information is then shared with others. That's one of the other principle objectives of science: to build a body of information that other people can rely on, for understanding both the present and the past, and also for driving the future forward.

There *is* a lot of really great innovation, engineering, and product development going on in the triathlon world and the related markets of swimming, biking, and running. And the companies doing that great work try really hard to explain it to you. *Faster* makes sure you'll get even more out of that information while also being able to spot the gimmicks. This book is designed to be as easy to read as the slick brochure selling you on the latest innovations—which may or may not be all that innovative. The only difference is that this book is not designed to sell you anything; it just wants to make you a smarter, *better* triathlete.

—Jordan Rapp
2011 ITU Long-Distance Triathlon World Champion
5-Time Ironman® Champion

PREFACE

I'VE BEEN A TECHNOLOGIST AND AN ENGINEER almost all of my life, a path that might have started with an obsession with Legos as a young child. From that time on, I've had jobs that focus on how to improve the way man-made objects interact with the physical world. As a cadet at the United States Air Force Academy, I helped assemble a satellite that was eventually launched into space and operated some of the first unmanned surveillance aircraft in the U.S. Army. So although I initially got into triathlon as a purely physical endeavor, it wasn't long before my natural inquisitiveness led me to approach it as exercise for my brain as well.

I did my first triathlon in 2004 and finished my first Iron-distance race four years later. Like most triathletes, I quickly developed a passion for the sport and sought all the information I could find to become a better athlete. I was surprised to discover the amount of research and development invested in triathlon equipment, training, and nutrition. From the shoes we wear to the bikes we ride to the techniques taught to us, our knowledge of the sport is furthered by discoveries made with the help of cutting-edge technology. My personal fascination with triathlon and science ultimately led me to a new profession.

I've written about the latest products and technological developments in cycling and triathlon for *LAVA, 3/GO Triathlon, 220 Triathlon, Triathlete, Inside Triathlon, Peloton,* and *Bicycle Times.* Through research and personal experience, I've learned some interesting things about the cultural and technological dynamics of triathlon. It takes extraordinary dedication and discipline for an athlete to compete in multiple races every year or to take the start line of an Iron-distance race. You train hard. You set high standards for yourself. You want to achieve your full potential. You want to go faster.

To serve triathletes like you, product manufacturers, coaches, and instructors push the technological boundaries of racing equipment and training methodologies far beyond what was thought possible a decade ago, and they continue to make new advances each year. The amount of scientific research that goes into endurance sports equipment today is staggering. This is a boon to dedicated athletes, but it has consequences as well. It's easy to become overwhelmed by the vast array of products advertising sophisticated research and technology. Meanwhile, there is very little information explaining the fundamental concepts underlying the rationale and development of these items. Additionally, as manufacturers make new discoveries at the cutting edge of aerodynamics and material science, it becomes ever more challenging for them to explain the value of their developments to athletes who do not have the requisite foundation in scientific knowledge. This has led to the emergence of gimmicks that market themselves with pseudoscience and obscure their effectiveness with doublespeak. Consequently, triathletes become frustrated, unable to maximize their gains in training and racing.

Triathletes need an understanding of the fundamental principles of racing technology, which can only be found piecemeal, buried in reams of advanced-level publications and journal articles. Instead of sorting through all this high-end data, they spend a significant amount of time searching the Internet to research products that will deliver performance—time they would rather spend swimming, cycling, or running. Often, they can't find a satisfactory answer online, leaving them to simply choose one of several expensive options without any guarantee of superior quality.

In short, it's hard for athletes to understand what makes the good stuff so good, and it's very easy for people making junk to fool you into thinking it's good. If triathletes could only find a way to capitalize on the scientific principles that are most beneficial to racing faster, they would likely discover that the good stuff is often the least expensive. There are endless magazine articles titled "Speed for Sale," and precious few with the title "Speed for *Free!*" Make no mistake. ***Free speed does exist. You just have to know where to find it.*** This book shows you some great places to look.

Faster bridges the technology gap for triathletes and points them to some non-equipment-based answers. Whether you're a newcomer to the sport, a gear hound who wants to get more educated about what goes into your equipment, an athlete on a budget looking to do more with less, or a serious competitor who wants to get every possible edge out of your training and gear, this book lays out the information you can use to obtain tangible results.

It's not as hard as you think. The prevailing myth in triathlon is that the science of speed is extremely complicated and difficult to understand. So triathletes go about their training neglecting the technological aspects of a sport that seem inaccessible. It's my goal to break down these concepts and make them easier to understand. Having spoken to many of the top product engineers and sports scientists around the world, I know that they can get carried away and quickly leave you behind with advanced ideas before establishing the fundamentals. Having taught high school math and science, I also know that the very idea of doing math and science is intimidating to some people. Let me reassure you, this isn't an attempt to make complicated things simple. The concepts aren't complicated in the first place. I have literally studied rocket science, and you have my professional assurance that ***this is not rocket science***.

For all the blood, sweat, and tears you put into your training so you can race harder, you owe it to yourself to do the homework that will help you race smarter. Don't let what you don't know hold you back from reaching your full potential. Instead, take a deep breath, grab your favorite recovery snack, give your legs a break, and get ready to pick up a few minutes on your finishing time by grabbing some scientific knowledge. Empower yourself to make smart choices in your equipment, training, and racing.

It's time to think about how you can go *faster*.

ACKNOWLEDGMENTS

Though this book's contents deal with science and technology, it has been a labor of love to put it together. I owe much to several friends and loved ones for their support, and I am indebted to an extraordinary number of great minds in sports science today who graciously shared their time and wisdom with me.

To my wife, Caroline, thank you for your patience and understanding as I burned the midnight oil. This was an endurance event, and you were, as always, my best aid station and encouragement.

To my son, Ethan, thanks for your continual fascination with this wondrous contraption called a bicycle, your boundless energy to run, and the unbridled joy you exhibit in water. Since you could crawl, you've been turning cranks on a bike with your hands and watching the chain and wheel move as a result. You remind me every day that the world is a beautiful place and that there exists infinite wonder in all things great and small.

I am eternally grateful to Jordan Rapp for his time, effort, and persistence in reviewing this work. Its quality is greatly enhanced by his professionalism and thoroughness. I am deeply honored that such a profound presence in the sport of triathlon became so involved in this.

There are not enough words to express my gratitude to Huub Toussaint for what he contributed to the information on swimming in this book. The book itself hardly does justice to the discoveries he's made on behalf of swimmers and triathletes the world over. Many thanks.

I took great inspiration and motivation from Matt Godo. His enthusiasm and contributions to cycling are tremendous, and I look forward to the fruits of his labors as he brings competitors the world over closer to the cutting edge of aerodynamic athletics.

To Renee Jardine of VeloPress, my gratitude for your patience and sincerity is matched only by the respect I have for your incredible professionalism. You are the editor who made this book better, the student who challenged me to become a better teacher, and the colleague who coached me to become a better writer.

And finally, to Jacob Norwood: I would never have become a writer if you had not encouraged me so strongly. Jacob had faith in me before I had it in myself. This is neither the first nor the last step on a long journey, but it is a big one and I owe much of my success in taking it to him. Thank you for your friendship now and always.

ACKNOWLEDGMENTS

CHAPTER 1

PHYSICS & THE TRIATHLETE

BEFORE WE BEGIN IN EARNEST, let's review some basic physics. The beginning of each chapter will refer back to these fundamental principles to get you into the right mind-set and help you see how science factors into swimming, cycling, and running.

BATTLE AGAINST THE UNIVERSE: FORCES AND HOW THEY RELATE TO YOU

Whether you're swimming, biking, or running, *there will always be two things involved: a body and a medium*. Though you might not have ever thought of it this way, your race is actually a battle against the universe. From the resistance of the water and the air to the earth's gravitational pull, *everything* is trying to keep you from moving forward. We cross finish lines all the time, and most of us hardly ever think about the fact that we've literally conquered heaven and earth to get there. But if you did think about it, you might find that you've been making things harder for yourself than they have to be.

Let's start by thinking about the human machine at rest. You are the **body**. On a bike, you and the bike are the body. You are surrounded by air. If you were to stand on the bottom of a pool, you'd be surrounded by water. As a swimmer in a triathlon, you are surrounded by a combination of air and water. In each case, you have to move through the air or the water. The **medium** is whatever the body moves through.

Your body has several scientific properties. You have a certain height, width, and depth. You have volume and surface area. You also possess a certain amount of mass, though this changes throughout the day according to your nutritional intake and conversion of that nutrition into energy. Let's describe a few of these physical properties in detail, beginning with mass.

Many people confuse the concept of mass with weight. **Mass** is a measurement of how much actual matter is in an object. Weight is a measurement of gravity's influence on that mass. To understand the difference, think of an astronaut orbiting the earth. She is weightless in space, but she still has the same mass. *Mass is matter, and weight is force.*

Next in order of importance to triathletes is **surface area**. Surface area is a major factor in aerodynamics, whether you are riding your bike or moving through the water. It also has a strong influence on an athlete's ability to dissipate heat during training and competition. If you inflate a balloon, the air entering the balloon will cause it to expand, increasing the total surface area. Oftentimes scientists deal with a specific region of an object's surface area, referred to simply as the **frontal area**. In aerodynamics, the frontal area is that part of the surface that first comes into contact with the fluid medium as it moves forward. There are other ways to change the surface and frontal area of an object. Hold your hands flat out in front of you. Now lay one over the top of the other. Notice how the palm of one hand is covering the back of the other, keeping both from being exposed to the air. You've just decreased the total surface area of your hands by almost half. Though human beings can only make slight adjustments to their surface area (not counting extreme weight loss), *they can make extraordinary changes by changing their body position*.

There's a further distinction that plays into aerodynamics in the water and on the bike. Although drag occurs across the entire surface area of a body, it is particularly influential on that part of your body that comes into contact with the air first, which we specified as the frontal area. Think of air molecules as paintballs. Would you rather be hit smack in the middle of your chest or have the ball break as it grazes your arm or hip? It's a lot less painful when the paintball skips off your skin, right? It's the same with wind and water, just on a much smaller scale. The best strategy is to duck down and make yourself as small as possible so fewer microscopic paintballs smack you straight on and more of them roll down your back. In fact, the most aerodynamic position you assume during a triathlon is in the water. Your frontal area is reduced to your head and shoulders, and a portion of your arms. Your torso and legs "draft" behind the rest of your body. It's why Superman flies head first. With that huge cape adding so much drag, he needs to be as efficient as possible! The most common way to reduce your frontal area is to lean farther over the aerobars on the bike or improve your streamline position in the water. Coaches and bike fitters go to great lengths to emphasize this, because *unnecessary frontal area significantly compromises performance*.

The property of **volume** and the associated principle of density become especially important in swimming performance. Think of your body as a giant container. If we filled it up with a given substance, how much would it hold? We could measure its capacity, or volume, in gallons, liters, or cubic inches. Now let's think back to the analogy of inflating a balloon. If you fill the balloon with helium, it will float up into the air. If you simply fill a balloon with air to make it the same size as the helium balloon, it will fall to the ground but float on water. Fill the balloon with sand, and it will sink in water. Helium, air, and sand have very different masses per unit of volume. When you divide an object's mass by its volume, you discover its **density**.

These are the fundamental physical properties of the body. The medium has the same properties, but because things like oceans and atmospheres are so large, we don't think of them in terms of their mass and volume. Instead, we are more concerned with the properties that influence bodies moving through them: viscosity, density, and the coefficient of friction. To get acquainted with these, let's take a closer look at how the body interacts with the medium.

Standing still is a pretty easy task, and we often take that simplicity for granted. But just because you're not moving doesn't mean your body is not exerting any effort. Gravity pulls down on you, and you have to exert a force to keep it from yanking you down onto the floor. If the wind blows or a current moves through the water, it will push you sideways until you exert another force to resist it. Forces like these are continually acting on us, and we exert a force against them, even when we are standing as shown in the figure on page 5. From this we can conclude two very important things about a body at rest:

- All forces act in direct opposition to each other.

- The forces combine to cancel each other out, and no net force results to move the object.

These two conditions are especially important to remember because they help us answer the triathlete's most-asked question: Why am I not going faster? All of this is summed up best in Newton's first law of motion: **A body at rest or in motion will tend to stay at rest or in motion unless a force acts on it.**

If your body didn't provide enough force to resist gravity, you'd fall to the ground. If there were no gravity, you'd remain still until you pushed down on the ground, and then you'd fly up into space. The same holds true for an object in motion. If you threw a baseball and no force of gravity or air resistance acted against it, it would keep going forever.

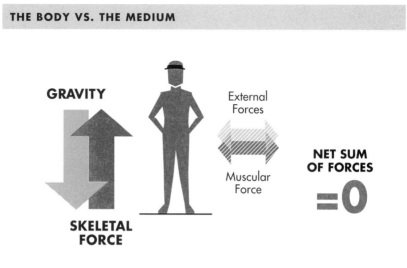

GRAVITY

External Forces

Muscular Force

SKELETAL FORCE

NET SUM OF FORCES

=0

Whether we're running or standing still, forces are constantly acting on us.

Let's examine the situation in more detail. Gravity exerts a force on you, pulling you down against the earth's surface. The surface itself holds you up when at rest and stops you cold whenever you fall, meaning it exerts a force in opposition to gravity. We all know but often forget that the skeleton exerts a force, too. Your foot bone is pulled down by gravity and pushed up by the ground; your leg bone is pulled down by gravity and pushed up by the foot bone; and the knee bone is pulled down by gravity and pushed up by the leg bone. So by singing the old "x-bone is connected to the y-bone" song and including forces, we see that the skeleton is an engineering marvel. At each point from the ground to the top of your head, wherever two surfaces come into contact, forces must be exerted to resist gravity. The earth's force is called the **gravitational force**. The force a body exerts against the surface upon which it rests is called the **normal force**. The normal force is always perpendicular to the surface and is equal to the force the object exerts directly against it. Whether it's bones, bike tires, or shoes, the same principle applies, and we'll see it constantly throughout this book.

The force the earth exerts on your skeleton is defined by the equation:

F = ma

*Where **F** is force, **m** is your body's mass (measured in kilograms, not pounds), and **a** is the rate of acceleration. For Earth's gravity, acceleration is 9.81 meters per second squared, or m/s².*

And with that equation explained, we now understand Newton's second law of motion: **The sum of the forces is equal to the mass of the body multiplied by its acceleration.**

In addition to force, you might recall that we have defined weight as a product of mass and gravity. In more rigorous terms, units of measurement such as pounds and ounces are measuring force. This is why you often see measurements of pressure or force in industrial equipment expressed in pounds. For consistency, we'll use the metric system throughout the book, though conversions are often noted to help you reference the units used on the racecourse. The metric unit of force, the newton (N), is, appropriately enough, named after the man who characterized it.

It may seem odd that it's your skeleton, not your muscles, doing the work to hold your body up, but it's true. That doesn't mean your muscles aren't also exerting a force. Quite the contrary, they're constantly making little twitches and gentle contractions to keep your skeleton perfectly balanced, just like you might use a finger to keep a house of cards balanced. It's the cards that are rigid enough to maintain an upright position, but it's your finger that prevents them from leaning one way or the other too much. That's an important distinction for triathletes, because as your muscles exert forces to move you, they change the amount of force placed on your bones and joints. The force is not always the same, and it's a big reason why some people tear muscles and others sprain ankles. Through the complicated interplay between muscles, tendons, and the impact of your foot against the ground, one force becomes too great for the others to compensate. Something's got to give, and in battles against Mother Nature we usually wind up on the short end of the stick. That brings us to Newton's third and final law: *For every action, there is an equal and opposite reaction.*

Problems arise when triathletes take Newton's third law for granted. Just to illustrate that point, consider this: You've never run a step in your life by pushing yourself. It's been the earth pushing you all this time.

Let's say a triathlete starts out at a run. *Wham!* His foot slams down on the pavement and his quads and glutes fire with maximum intensity. Watch the earth go! That's right, the earth. That's what our triathlete is trying to move, isn't he? He's exerting a muscular force, pushing down on our planet. Didn't see it move much, did you? The earth is obeying Newton's first law: The force exerted against it isn't sufficient to disturb it from its original motion. However, that doesn't excuse it from adhering to Newton's third law. A force has been exerted on it. It has to return the favor. If the earth won't be pushed down, then the triathlete must be pushed up. The triathlete gets just about all of his muscular energy returned to him in the form of forward motion. *Boom!* He's off and running.

The same goes for cycling, though the force the leg applies is transferred a few times before reaching the ground. The wheels on our bikes go round and round, but the earth continues to spin on its axis without interruption. Down the road we go.

GET A GRIP: THE IMPORTANCE OF FRICTION

We take it for granted that we don't slip and fall every time we step out on a run or roll out on our bikes. There's a very important physical principle that prevents us from eating pavement. Strangely enough, as helpful as it is, we're constantly trying to find new ways to beat it. That physical principle is called **friction**.

Friction isn't a thing, it's an interaction between two things. When your shoe or tire hits the pavement, the two surfaces rub and scrape against each other, and not just in terms of your tread pattern on gravel. Although the visible texture of the two surfaces matters, friction actually occurs at the molecular level. That's why we use highly polished metal skates to slide along ice, and pedal extra carefully along rainy streets. Several factors influence just how much friction we experience: material composition, temperature, and the physical state of the matter. All of this is measured experimentally and can then be summed up in one number, called the coefficient of friction (expressed by the Greek letter μ). There are no units for the coefficient of friction. It is said to be dimensionless. As a general rule, it's best to keep the coefficient of friction as low as possible. Scientists have done enough research over time to create a list of coefficients of friction for different materials. For instance, bicycle tires typically have a value between 0.0025 and 0.005.

The biggest factor influencing terrestrial friction is the mass of the object in contact with the ground. We see this relationship in the equation for friction:

$$F_f = \mu mg$$

*Where **m** is the mass of the object, **g** is the force of gravity and **μ** (pronounced "mew") is the coefficient of friction.*

The **coefficient of friction** describes just how much two materials (like rubber and asphalt) will want to resist moving past each other. The actual friction depends on how they're applied to each other. Since normal force is equal to mass multiplied by gravity, we simply say

$$F_f = \mu F_N$$

Where F_N equals normal force.

This equation will become important when we talk about the relative value of saving weight on bicycle components in Chapter 3.

FEEL THE FLOW: AN INTRODUCTION TO AERODYNAMICS

You may have heard the phrase "Nature abhors a vacuum." That's why it's filled with things like air and water. Every time you pour on the steam in a race, you're performing the equivalent of shoving your way through a subway crowd of microscopic molecules. Oxygen, hydrogen, carbon, and nitrogen are all in your face, and as good as it might feel to have them blowing through your hair, they're actually shoving back against you. You start to press your way through the crowd without so much as an "Excuse me." As you pass by them, they turn around and pull on you. Push, scrape, and pull: Those molecules catch you in three different ways, and the faster you try to go, the harder they're going to resist. This is what we call **drag**. Product manufacturers are constantly selling revolutionary technologies to help you beat drag. However, there's a lot you can do to cut down on drag without spending a dime, and there are even a few things you can do to take advantage of drag. We'll get into that in more detail as we hit the specifics of each discipline within the sport, but for now let's get a handle on the concept of drag.

Depending on who you are and how you move through that subway car, you'll get different reactions from the people you pass. People step aside politely for a pregnant woman, shove back against an angry line-backer trying to throw his weight around, and reach out and grab a thief by his large jacket or the purse he just stole. The size, speed, and shape of these folks is a very good analogy for aerodynamics, because air doesn't react the same way to all objects.

Because the atmosphere acts on different bodies in different ways, knowing the different kinds of drag will help us guess which ones will act on feathers, hammers, and triathletes. Meet the Drag family:

Pressure drag (also called form drag) is the version we are most familiar with. You try to move forward and occupy the space taken up by air molecules. The easiest thing for them to do would be to back away from you, except for the fact that there are miles and miles of other molecules behind them. What happens is a big mashup, and the molecules are forced to push up against you. The faster you try to move, the more molecules get pressed against the crowd behind them, and the more resistance they encounter from all the molecules behind them. All this pushing and shoving generates a lot of pressure, so the only option you leave these poor molecules is to squeeze around you to let you by. As you go past them, those molecules are desperate to return to their previous position. So they rush back in and fill the vacuum behind you. Because there are millions of these molecules, it's a very chaotic scene and they swirl about in all directions, creating a phenomenon known as a **vortex**.

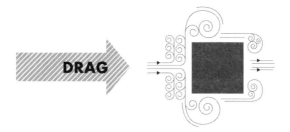

In your case, they create several vortices. These vortices are like tiny tornadoes, sucking in anything near them, including you. You're stronger than these tornadoes, of course, but you still feel the effect. Remember how molecules shoving against your frontal area created a region of high pressure? The vortices are a region of *low* pressure. That pressure difference means air is pushing *and* pulling you backward. The faster you try to go, the harder it gets because you've got more molecules working on you at once. Since this type of drag is the result of a collision between the front of your body and the air, it stands to reason that the bigger your frontal area, the more drag you'll face. On the subway, the bigger our linebacker is, the more people he's going to shove as he moves through the car. There's a direct relationship between his size and the resistance he faces. It's the same for you and those air molecules. It's kind of tough to get smaller, but there are still ways to beat pressure drag. Those ways are best exemplified by our pregnant woman. As soon as she steps into the subway car, people take notice and move aside for her. She doesn't have to say, "Excuse me, I'm pregnant." The shape of her belly tells everyone all they need to know, and they react politely to that shape by offering less resistance. Air is the same way. Certain shapes get a more "polite" reaction from air molecules. The teardrop design of time trial helmets says "Pardon me" to the atmosphere, and the molecules bend less chaotically around it and create fewer vortices. More on that later.

Skin friction drag describes the resistance you encounter as those air molecules move around you. Typically in triathlon we don't have to worry about this too much: Engineers consider the influence of skin friction drag on highly polished bikes and skin-tight jerseys negligible. However, let's briefly explore it for the sake of being thorough. Imagine that our thief tries to run through the subway car as someone shouts, "Stop that man!" If the thief is clutching the purse he just stole to his chest, then the purse adds to his pressure drag. We essentially consider the purse a part of his frontal area. But what if he's carrying it by the shoulder strap? That bag is flapping all over the place, just begging to be grabbed by one of the passengers. It's the same way with your own equipment. Wear a baggy running shirt, unzip your jersey, or attach your race number to your bike carelessly, and they flap around. All these little odds and ends hanging off you don't necessarily add much to your surface area, but they give air molecules a little something extra to grab on to.

Induced drag takes into account how you approach the air. Whereas with pressure drag and skin friction drag we were focused more on size and texture of our surface area, here we consider how our orientation changes our frontal area. This is no small consideration for triathletes, since we gradually change that orientation throughout the course of a race. We begin the swim completely horizontal, almost flying through the water like Superman flies through air (if only that were true!). We spend our time on the bike sitting in a hunched-over position, and then we finally stand fully upright to run. Our orientation to our direction of motion, and consequently the direction of air or water flow, goes from parallel to perpendicular in the span of two transition areas. The change in that orientation changes the relative surface area of our bodies that is exposed to the elements, as shown in the figure on page 13. Aerodynamicists refer to that orientation as **angle of attack**. At a higher angle of attack, you expose a greater percentage of surface area to the air or water, and this can induce a greater amount of pressure drag. That's why we call it induced drag.[1]

FASTER

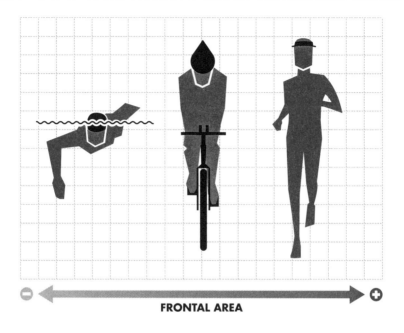

FRONTAL AREA

During the course of the race, an athlete's angle of attack increases, exposing more area to air resistance.

We know that an object's size, speed, shape, orientation, and the density of the medium it moves through will all affect how fast the object is able to move. Scientists have taken those variables and used them to create a formula for describing just how efficiently an object will move through the air or water. That relative efficiency is called the **drag coefficient (C_d)**, and it's expressed by the following equation:[2]

$$C_d = \frac{D}{\rho \times v^2 \times \frac{A}{2}}$$

*Where **D** is the observed drag, **ρ** is the fluid field density, **v** is the object's velocity, and **A** is the frontal surface area.*

Given that we're talking about velocity and an observed level of drag, some experimentation in the lab is necessary to figure out an object's drag coefficient. Thankfully, the good folks at NASA and other research institutions have been performing these kinds of experiments for years, and so we have data on a wide range of shapes. Here are a few:[3]

OBJECT	C_d
Flat Plate	1.28
Runner	0.8–0.9
Prism	1.14
Cyclist on a Bike	0.5–0.7
Sphere	0.5
Elite Swimmer	0.4–0.5
Airfoil	0.045

We can see that flat, wide objects have a higher drag coefficient and tapered, narrow objects have a lower coefficient. Because of our relative size and shape, triathletes are on the higher end of the spectrum, but we can adapt our positioning and accessories to overcome some of that. From swimming to running, you make a change in your angle of attack by almost 90 degrees, and it just about doubles your cost in drag.

That about wraps up our introduction to the science of your race. There will be a few other concepts we'll introduce along the way, but these are the fundamental principles that apply to just about every discipline of your triathlon effort. Nothing can be overly complicated so long as you remember how scientists unlocked these principles of physics in the first place—by reducing the problems to their most basic forms and observing things one step at a time. If you feel like some of the items discussed here were oversimplified, don't sweat it. Developing the most beneficial relationship between yourself and the physical universe involves several factors, and there is no end of tips and tools being offered to triathletes by the endurance sports market. Using the most effective tools and methods requires a solid understanding of the basics. Now that we have the fundamentals in hand, it's time to see how we can apply them to our advantage. Knowing the ways your body and the earth's medium work in relation to each other is the surest way to get the two interacting in smoother— and faster—fashion. Having sized up all that's working against you, we're ready to develop a strategy to overcome it.

THE SWIM

THE SWIM IS THE SHORTEST LEG OF A TRIATHLON, but unless the rest of the race goes up Mount Everest, it feels like it takes the greatest exertion to get through the water. You are already intuitively aware of the reason why: Water is thicker than air, and so it produces a great deal of resistance against us as we try to move through it. Making matters worse, though water is thicker than air, it's less solid than the ground, so it doesn't do us the favor of holding us up as we go. Swimmers therefore face the double whammy of moving through a medium that pushes hard against them but does nothing to keep them from drowning. The universe is out to get us!

Fortunately, we're equipped to overcome this obstacle. Given our large brains, humans figured out long ago that we don't need fins and gills to swim. We just need proper technique. Instead of trying to walk along the bottom of a lake for 1.2 or 2.4 miles at a time, we stretched ourselves out flat and began to kick our legs and pull with our arms, significantly decreasing our induced drag. But have you ever really stopped to think about it? Swimming . . . how does *that* work?

Lucky for us, a lot of really smart scientists and engineers have spent their careers thinking about swimming, and they have found answers to the questions triathletes most often ask (or should ask) about it. Our exploration of the subject begins exactly where theirs did: with the body and the medium.

EVERYBODY IN THE WATER: THE BODY & THE MEDIUM

In Chapter 1 we compared the swimming triathlete to Superman flying through the air. In actuality, there isn't much difference between the two. Other than the effect its density has on speed, water behaves almost exactly the same as air. All of the forces that keep airplanes and birds from crashing to the ground also keep you from sinking in the water. Let's take a look at those things in detail.

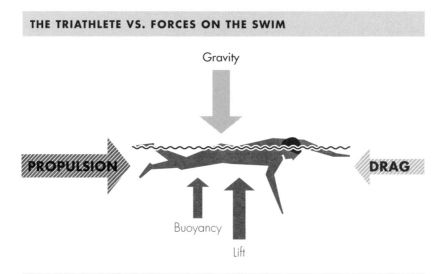

THE TRIATHLETE VS. FORCES ON THE SWIM

Gravity

PROPULSION

DRAG

Buoyancy

Lift

Forces act in four primary directions regardless of the medium. The net force in the vertical direction is zero. The net force in the horizontal direction is positive, creating forward acceleration.

Just as in flight, *there are always four forces acting on a body in water: weight, lift, drag, and propulsion*—with one exception. An airplane has to move forward to create lift, but a human body in water doesn't necessarily have to maintain forward motion to float. That's because our ability to stay up is partially based on **buoyancy**, which is defined as a body's tendency to float when submerged in water. In that regard, people behave partly like a blimp and partly like an airplane in the water. Take a moment to imagine a machine that's half blimp and half airplane. Any way you cut it, it's a pretty clumsy-looking vehicle, isn't it? That may actually validate the analogy.

The water is the environment in which we are the slowest and most awkward. Human beings can maintain good running or cycling form at a range of speeds, but we're much more limited in the water. Go too fast or too slow, and things start to fall apart. A great deal of that has to do with the four forces acting on us and how we interact with them. Let's examine the body and the medium by breaking them down according to those forces.

Weight

Weight initially seems like an obvious concept to understand. You are heavier than water, so you sink. But there's a slight nuance involved that we need to examine in order to fully understand the next concept, buoyancy. We don't want to confuse mass with weight. Remember that mass measures the amount of matter in your body, and weight measures the force exerted on it by gravity. Once we start a race, the concept of the earth exerting a force on your body becomes of paramount concern.

Buoyancy & Lift

When an object begins to settle in water, it pushes that water out of its way in a process known as **displacement**. The amount of water the object displaces is equal to its volume. That volume of water has a certain amount of mass.

Moving that mass of water requires a force. If the object is removed from the water, the water immediately moves back in to fill the space it occupied. Moving back in requires the same amount of force it took to displace the water in the first place, and since the water moves instantly, we can conclude that the force is being exerted constantly. There's a way to determine the magnitude of that force. If we knew the exact volume of the water, we would know its mass. According to Newton's laws, the amount of force that mass exerts is

$F = ma$

Where a equals 9.81 m/s^2.

Or, in other words, the *weight* of the water.

So the force the water exerts is equal to the weight of the volume that was displaced. It's important to understand that the force of water pushing up on you as you swim is dependent on your volume, not your weight. This is how a multi-ton boat can stay afloat: Its hull displaces enough water to create sufficient force to hold the weight up. Let's consider this principle on a smaller scale. We drop a rubber duck and a rock of equal size into water at the same time. The duck floats. The rock doesn't. Both objects displace the same volume of water and encounter the same amount of gravity, but the rock has more mass. Because the rock exerts more force on the water, it overcomes the upward force, or **lift**. The duck exerts less force in proportion to its displacement, so it floats.

Our lungs fill with air, making us a little like that rubber duck, or a blimp. That air doesn't give us everything we need to stay up, though, so we have to swim to keep from sinking. We're quite familiar with this from practical experience, but understanding the theory is still important. If all of your kicking and arm paddling is directed in the lateral, or forward, direction, then where does the lift come from? How does motion translate into floatation?

Here is the fundamental principle: ***Any time a body moves through a fluid, that fluid will exert two forces on it as a result of its interaction***

with the body. Those two forces are lift and drag. That's it. Two forces: one perpendicular, one parallel. There are no in-betweens. Whether it's a swimmer, a set of water skis, a brick, or an airplane wing, the principle is the same. We can easily see how this works by using an **airfoil**, a familiar shape in aerodynamics and triathlon that looks like the cross section of a wing.

Here we see the concept in action. Water moves over and under the airfoil shape. When everything is nice and symmetrical, the water moving over the top and the bottom travel at the same rate and particles meet back up at the tail in an orderly fashion to fill the vacuum left by the airfoil. However, once the airfoil either becomes asymmetrical or increases its angle of attack, the system begins to destabilize.

Now we see that the water moving over the airfoil has to travel farther than the water moving underneath it, so that top water has to go faster in order to rejoin the molecules it was separated from. This faster motion creates lower pressure above the airfoil than beneath it (see the vortex?), and when the pressure underneath is higher, you have an imbalance in the forces acting

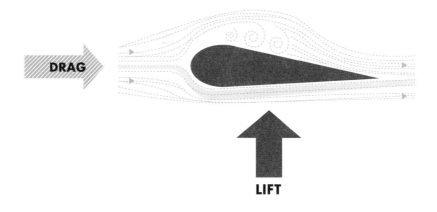

on the airfoil, or in the case of a swimmer, the body. This is called **Bernoulli's principle**, named after the Italian scientist who discovered its occurrence.[1]

This imbalance in pressure creates a force that pushes the body up. This force is magnified by the fact that you don't swim completely submerged. Triathletes try to keep as much of their bodies out of the water as possible, and because of that the amount of water running over their backs is much smaller than the amount running underneath them. What's on top is air, and the air pressure pushing down is at a much lower pressure than the water pressure pushing up. *Lift always acts exactly perpendicular to the body's weight. Drag force always acts against the body's direction of motion, or propulsion.*[2]

Drag

The drag involved in propulsion is pressure drag, which is caused by an imbalance in the pressure on opposite sides of a body's surface. Induced drag and skin friction drag are also at work in the water, though pressure drag makes up the overwhelming majority of total drag force.

Because water has a greater density than air, it does not move as easily around a body pushing through it. This gives rise to other types of drag that act on swimmers. The second most influential type is called **wave drag**. This occurs when the body of a swimmer moves so fast that water actually moves backward to stay ahead of the swimmer instead of passing over his body. As it "backpedals," this water can't take up the space already filled by the molecules behind it, so it piles up on top of them. This causes a wave to form in front of the swimmer. The wave is an extra mass of water in front of him, and as he moves faster, he can actually begin to overtake it. Doing so creates a strong resistive force and hinders speed further. There's good news, though—if you want to call it that. Triathletes don't actually swim fast enough for wave drag to be a significant factor.

Research indicates that a swimmer has to move through the water at 1.7 meters per second (m/s) before wave drag accounts for 10 percent of total

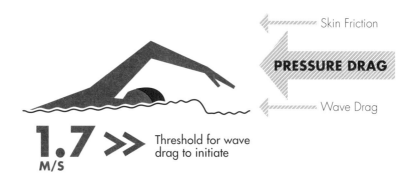

Skin Friction

PRESSURE DRAG

Wave Drag

1.7 **>>** Threshold for wave
M/S drag to initiate

Note the wave surging just in front of the swimmer's head. This shows the region of high pressure building in front that contributes to drag.

drag.[3] That being the case, wave drag appears to be a concern for only the world's fastest and most dedicated Olympic swimmers. To compare, let's take a look at the speeds clocked by the world's top swimmers in and out of the pool:

Michael Phelps's Olympic record 200-m freestyle[4]   1.94 m/s
Oussama Mellouli's winning 10-km marathon swim
    at the 2012 London Olympics[5]   1.52 m/s
Top elites in an Olympic-distance triathlon[6] (17:00)   1.47 m/s
Andy Potts's winning time in a 70.3[7]   1.37 m/s
Lars Jorgensen's Kona course record[8]   1.37 m/s

It may look like they're close, but pressure drag is proportionate to the *cube* of a swimmer's velocity, which means you pick up a lot more drag for just a small increase in speed. Three-tenths (0.3) of a meter per second is actually a significant speed gap as far as water is concerned, and 1.7 m/s remains a firm threshold for wave drag to initiate.[9] It would take an unprecedented level of effort before wave drag became a concern for triathlon's top swimmers. For the rest of us average humans, it will never be a problem, meaning pressure drag is the only thing we should worry about.

The final form of drag that is sometimes mentioned in swimming technology is known as skin friction drag, as you might recall from our subway purse thief example from Chapter 1. There have been attempts to introduce technologies that reduce overall drag by defeating skin friction drag on a swimmer. The relative effectiveness of those innovative attempts will be discussed later in this chapter, but first let's put the overall contribution of skin friction drag to a swimmer's performance into perspective.

Computer models of swimmers moving through water (the same technologies that are used to create more-aerodynamic bikes) have assessed the amount of drag caused as water passes over the skin of an athlete. The models reveal two interesting things. First, skin friction drag does not seem to be as dependent upon a swimmer's speed as wave or pressure drag are. It does change somewhat as swimming velocity approaches 2.0 m/s, and, in fact, skin friction drag actually *decreases* at that point.[10] The decrease is negligible, however, because it's a very small change in an already small number, not to mention that you'd need a propeller to reach that speed. However, skin friction drag's *relative* contribution to a swimmer's total drag is a little more difficult to pin down as compared to pressure drag, which changes much more radically with respect to speed and body position. When a swimmer holds both arms out in front of her in a gliding position, for example, her pressure drag is significantly reduced and skin friction drag actually makes up about 13 percent of her total drag in the water. When she glides with her arms at her side, however, pressure drag increases significantly and friction drag accounts for about 8 percent of her total drag.[11] Because triathletes are in constant motion and their arms never lock in a glide position, it is likely that skin friction drag values lie somewhere between these two extremes.

In the grand scheme of things, it's safe for triathletes to assume that pressure drag makes up 80 percent of the total resistive force, with wave drag and friction drag each contributing approximately 10 percent each. *So stop worrying about wave drag and skin friction drag, and focus on reducing pressure drag.*

Propulsion (Thrust)

The propulsive forces are easily understandable in basic terms, but there's a caveat to propulsion in swimming that has a big impact on speed. That caveat is the entire reason we move so much more slowly in the water than anywhere else. Too many people conclude that water's density is the only reason we're slower; it's also a key component helping us move.

Propulsion is all about drag. You push your arm back against water. That water has to move out of the way to allow your hand to come through. This leaves a vortex on the back side of your hand and arm. Water rushes around your arm to fill that void, creating a pressure difference. Once again, we get drag, but now the drag is oriented in the direction you're trying to

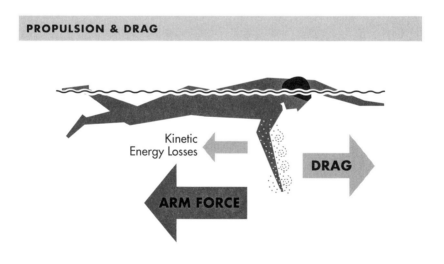

PROPULSION & DRAG

Kinetic Energy Losses

DRAG

ARM FORCE

A closer look at the catch shows that the force the arm creates mostly accelerates the water backward.

go. In this case, you're "dragging" yourself straight ahead! However, it's not that simple. The water doesn't just move around to the back side of your hand. It has other places to be, and it gladly receives the push you give it and continues on its way. In other words, a significant amount of your arm's muscular effort goes toward accelerating water backwards instead of moving you forward. That acceleration means kinetic energy is transferred from your arm to the water. No wonder you feel so tired after a hard race effort: Water drains your energy in all kinds of ways!

Scientists have developed sophisticated mechanisms to measure the drag of a swimmer's body and the propulsive force a person generates while swimming. They characterize their measurements in terms of efficiency. In other words, they observe how much force is "wasted" on overcoming drag and transferring kinetic energy to the water versus how much force actually goes toward moving you through the water. Expressed mathematically as a percentage, it looks like this:[12]

$$Eff = \frac{F_D}{F_K + F_D}$$

Where **Eff** is efficiency, F_D is the force necessary to overcome drag, and F_K is the force lost as a transfer of kinetic energy to the water.

From their studies, scientists have found the following propulsive efficiency factors for different "species" moving through water at their maximum speed.[13]

Fish	80%
Competitive Swimmers	61%
Triathletes	44%

It may sound funny to think of swimmers and triathletes as totally different animals, but just looking at their relative efficiencies makes it difficult to believe two groups of human beings can be so different.

That difference is further emphasized by data collected on physiological performance during swimming. At an equal level of oxygen uptake, dedicated swimmers are 23 percent faster. In other words, their advantage over triathletes has very little to do with greater strength or endurance as a result of more focused training.[14] This is a great example of the need to understand the science of triathlon and the ultimate benefit of knowing the fundamental concepts behind things like propulsion. These numbers prove in black and white what coaches have been telling triathletes for years: *Technique matters.*

Research indicates that superior triathlon swimmers such as Andy Potts and Julie Dibens owe very little of their edge to some advantage in upper body strength or unique body proportions. (Even though scientists have indicated Michael Phelps's anatomy is particularly suited to swimming, it still accounts for only a fractional advantage.) Their real benefit comes from years spent training technique in the pool. In fact, studies show that propulsive efficiency encompasses the orientation and path of the *entire arm* as it moves through the water. A single arm pulling through the water while swimming is a highly complex system. There are multiple points of articulation in the arm that transfer energy and influence movement through a chaotic fluid environment against which the hand exerts force in an effort to generate the greatest possible propulsion. Everything is connected to everything, and if any one piece of the system falls out of place, the whole thing breaks down.

You might have noticed that our entire discussion about propulsion so far has centered on the arms. What about the legs? As it turns out, a swimmer's kick only contributes about 10 to 15 percent of the total propulsion. In the case of a poorly trained swimmer (*Cough! Triathletes! Cough-cough!*), the contribution can dip even lower. That's no reason to ignore proper kicking technique, however, because of what the kick does accomplish when performed correctly and what it can do when performed the wrong way.

To understand why kicking is such an inefficient propulsive method yet such an important motion, we need to consider the nature of the leg's shape and movement. From your hip to your ankle, your leg is pretty much shaped like a cylinder. Your foot is shaped more like a flat plate. Put them together and the best analogy for the leg is a long spoon. If we stick a spoon into a pitcher of water and stir, we'll see a whirlpool form as we stir faster. But what if we just have a stick? We would have to stir much faster in order to create a whirlpool. This is the problem with our legs when it comes to swimming. Our feet are too small to take advantage of our leg power. Take one look at a duck or frog at your local pond, and you will see just how woefully equipped humans are for leg-based propulsion by comparison.

We can't throw kicking out with the pool water, though. Grab a pull buoy, and you will understand why soon enough. When you stop kicking, the buoy keeps your hips and thighs from sinking. It works according to the principle of buoyancy. Kicking also keeps your hips up by contributing to the body's overall lift. It's that dual blimp-airplane nature of the human body at work that we talked about earlier. Practicing your technique maximizes lift and keeps your body horizontal in the water, which reduces drag. But proper kicking technique keeps drag low in other ways, too.

VERTICAL FORCES IN KICKING

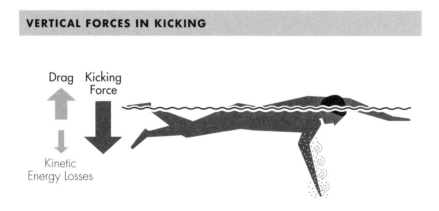

The force generated from kicking doesn't contribute as much to propulsion as your arm movements, but it improves the body's overall lift, which ultimately reduces drag. This reduces the angle of attack, cutting induced drag.

FASTER

Let's revisit our spoon analogy. We know that moving a spoon through the water at a perpendicular angle is the most effective way to get the water moving (think of stirring a pitcher of lemonade), but it requires a relatively strong force. The easiest way for the spoon to cut through water would be to run it lengthwise. Similarly, the leg's profile is much smaller when it's parallel to the direction of travel and presents less surface area in direct opposition to the water. That's only the case so long as the leg remains straight, though. Once the leg begins to bend, it presents more surface area for water to push against. You get more drag.

These are just the very basic principles of swimming propulsion. Scientists have conducted elaborate studies and made discoveries about swimming technique that would require much more space to explain than is available here, and much of it is difficult to put into practice without world-class coaching and state-of-the-art analysis tools such as those found in Olympic training centers. But there are a couple of questions that science can answer to the triathlete's benefit. Let's take a look at those.

CATCHING A CLUE: IS IT BETTER TO CUP YOUR HANDS OR KEEP THEM FLAT?

This is a question that seems easy at first, is made complicated if you think about it enough, and then gets simple again after you *really* think about it. Let's say you get to your masters class early one day so you decide to splash around in the water a bit. You move your hand through the water in a sweeping motion (otherwise known as sculling), getting a feel for the water resistance against your hand. Like sticking your hand out the car window, changing the pitch and force of your arm produces different results and sensations. It seems like your hand is acting the same way as an airplane wing. And then it occurs to you:

"Hey, airplane wings are curved . . . maybe I should curve my hand to simulate that shape."

Another comparison is to make your hand look like a parachute, cupping it slightly while swimming. Both examples speak to the idea behind Bernoulli's principle, which we discussed on page 22. Cupping the hand creates a curvature and requires air to travel farther over it than water traveling under it, which creates a pressure difference. It would seem that this should allow us to get more propulsion through the water. It's a great idea and a fine attempt to apply science. It's just that it doesn't work in this case.

Without getting deep into the mathematics, here's why. A parachute succeeds in using Bernoulli's principle for three reasons. First, a parachute has a large surface area to "catch" air. Second, while the skydiver uses the chute to slow her descent, the chute is using the skydiver to provide enough downward acceleration to maintain speed. If the parachute moved too slowly, it would collapse. That leads to the third reason for the success of Bernoulli's principle in this scenario. Air has a certain density, and the parachute is designed to work in atmosphere of a certain consistency. When the air gets too thin, it won't work. We see this happen in skydiving accidents when two jumpers overlap each other. The lower parachute "steals" air, and the higher one collapses.

So, to relate Bernoulli's principle back to a parachute-shaped hand in swimming, a triathlete requires three things to make the system work: surface area, speed, and density. Water certainly provides the density, but mathematical analysis shows that a human being can't produce enough speed or surface area with her hand to make Bernoulli's principle work.[15] Whether you can feel it or not, your "parachute," i.e., hand, is collapsing as you pull your way through the water. But never fear, there's still a way to catch more water: by letting it slip through your fingers.

Your hand isn't large enough or fast enough to let you generate a sufficient *lift* force when it's cupped. But the hand is obviously working against *some* kind of force, and if it isn't lift, that only leaves drag. Sure enough, that's the dominant force at work, and if we can maximize it then we can effectively give our hands something extra to push against. With more to push against, we transfer less of our energy into the water and more of it into useful propulsion.

If you want to be a better swimmer, you'll seek out ways to increase drag on your hands. There are a couple of ways to do it. Increasing the speed that your hands move through the water will help, but hopefully you're already working on that in training. Another method to increase drag would be to increase the surface area of your hands. Racecourse officials frown upon the use of hand paddles, but there's another small trick that yields a big bonus. Drag occurs when vortices form on the trailing edge of a surface (in this case, the back of your hand) and create a pressure difference. So what we want to achieve is a structure that creates more vortices.[16] Think back to our spoon model. What if we put slots in the spoon to let the water pass through? By spreading our fingers out just slightly, we can achieve a similar effect.

Using computer-generated models, scientists have found that an approximate separation of 12 degrees (or 8 millimeters between fingertips) increases the drag coefficient of the hand by nearly 9 percent.[17] That doesn't correspond to a similar increase in propulsive efficiency, but it's certainly a remarkable gain!

FISHTAILING: THE BENEFIT OF DRAFTING OTHER SWIMMERS

Drafting: It's a dirty word on the bike course, but hardly an avoidable situation in the large mass starts of a triathlon. With all the slapping and fighting that occurs in the initial stages of a triathlon swim, athletes find reason to consider if it would be better to make a break for it and try to get out front or to settle in behind someone who seems to be doing well and just stay on their feet until someone else passes. Tactically, the latter is a dubious proposition, because you never know the ability level of the person in front of you. But scientifically, there are very good arguments for trying it. Sometimes there are advantages to being *second*-fastest.

There have been multiple studies on the subject of drafting in swimming, both in computer simulations and controlled aquatic environments. Granted, neither one is the real world, where the chaotic nature of waves and competitors changes things in ways we can't predict. But based on the data that's been collected, we have reasonable assurance that riding the wake of another swimmer has benefits.

Regardless of their analytical methods, researchers generally agree that you have to be within 50 centimeters (1.6 feet) of your unwitting assistant to maximize the draft advantage. Computer models suggest that you might still experience a drag reduction of 30 percent at a distance of 3.5 meters (11.5 feet), but these assume ideal (read: "pool") conditions and speeds not usually seen in triathlons except by professionals. Assuming you are swimming among athletes of equal size who maintain their spacing at constant velocity, your drag is reduced by approximately 40 percent or more when you close the distance to a meter or less.[18] That's obviously an extreme challenge for any athlete, but especially the age grouper struggling for space in a pack of possibly hundreds. Your savings are nullified if your hands continually hit the feet of the person in front of you. Other research shows there's an easier way to do it. The figure on page 33 shows that with a lateral offset of 1 meter (3.3 feet) and by adjusting your spacing so your hand enters the water approximately even with your leader's shoulders, you can still reduce your drag by up to 20 percent (assuming you are swimming with swimmers of equal size).[19]

Although the relationship between reduced drag and its savings on actual physical effort can't be definitively charted, several studies on the intensity of effort during swimming suggest that drafting in the water can not only save you time but can also delay muscular fatigue. In one test, scientists asked triathletes to swim a 750-meter trial at a constant speed in both the lead and draft positions. The results indicated that drafting swimmers experienced heart rates approximately 10 beats per minute slower and an approximate 2 millimole reduction in blood

LATERAL DRAFTING POSITION

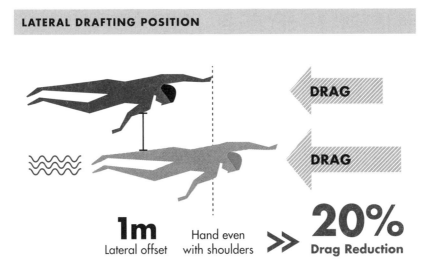

1m Hand even
Lateral offset with shoulders

DRAG

DRAG

>> 20%
Drag Reduction

Drafting during the swim can substantially ease your physiological effort, leading to further benefits during the bike and the run. Due to the greater density of water, the effect of drafting is more pronounced even at substantially lower speeds.

lactate concentration.[20] These savings pay dividends long after the first transition. Finding a way to get through the water with less effort carries over to the bike and possibly even to the running phase of the race. In another study, scientists asked triathletes to complete a 750-meter swim, 20-km bike, and 5-km run at swim intensities of 80–85 percent, 90–95 percent, and 100 percent of their maximum effort. The results indicated that power output on the bike was reduced as the intensity of the swim effort increased. Additionally, athletes in the 80–85 percent group had a 1 percent faster run time than the maximum-effort swimmers. The result was that the swimmers with the lowest swim effort actually finished the triathlon about 1:45 faster than the maximum-intensity group.[21]

SALTY DOGS & FLASH FREEZES: IS THERE REALLY SUCH A THING AS "FAST" WATER?

It ought to be pretty intuitive to any triathlete who's ever swum in a wet suit that it provides a significant speed advantage in the water. Of course, you need the water to be a certain temperature before wet suits are legal, let alone advisable. So what about non-wet-suit conditions? If you're going to swim in warmer water, does a much warmer temperature benefit you? What about ocean versus fresh water? People float easier in the Dead Sea because of its salt content. But does all that salt add more drag? Is there "fast water," and if so, where can we find it?

The argument about how drag and lift affect swimmers is no small thing. Its origins go all the way back to the 1600s, when Isaac Newton was writing his *Principia Mathematica*. In addition to describing gravity and the laws of motion, he also examined objects moving through fluids. In the process, he made the observation that it was harder to stir a pot of molasses than a pot of water, and that stirring a pot of air was even easier. It stood to reason, in his view, that the major factor in a fluid's resistance is its **viscosity**, otherwise known as the "stickiness" of the fluid. He therefore hypothesized that the major component of resistive force to a body moving through a fluid is skin friction drag.

That's when Christiaan Huygens came along. Huygens, a Dutch contemporary of Newton, was a fairly big-brained individual who helped create calculus when he wasn't busy doing things like discovering Saturn's moons or inventing the grandfather clock. So Newton listened when Huygens disputed his hypothesis. Huygens believed that pressure drag would take the greatest toll on a body based on the fluid's density. Newton couldn't decide, so he split the difference and wrote both arguments into his book, which led to confusion and frustration among swimming coaches and triathletes centuries later.

It wasn't until nearly four hundred years after Newton's death that we finally got a verdict. In 2006, Professor Edward Cussler of the University of Minnesota set out to resolve the debate once and for all. He poured 300 kilograms of guar gum (a thickening agent used in condiments) into the school's swimming pool, then told a squad of volunteers to hop in and swim. After several 25-meter laps in both gummy and clean pools, Cussler and his team concluded that viscosity had no impact on a swimmer's performance. They knew that viscosity was the only factor that had radically changed with the addition of the guar gum, which didn't have a significant impact on the water's density. All things being equal, you can swim just as fast in really sticky water as you can in pure water.[22] But why?

It all comes down to the fact that even when it seems the universe has stacked the deck against you, it has to obey its own laws. Remember: A drag force always acts against a body's direction of motion or propulsion. Water, in all its dense and "sticky" glory, opposes your body's forward motion, but it must give equal opposition to the backward motion of your hands and feet. Though the thicker water is more difficult for your body to move through, it also gives you more substance to push your hand against. Temperature or salinity will never make the water as viscous as adding guar gum to it. Just for reference, take a look at this graph.

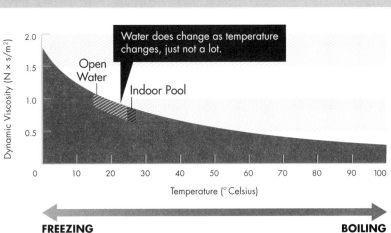

Water *does* change as its temperature changes, just not a lot. The difference in viscosity between boiling water and freezing water is a factor of about 0.0018. That's *tiny*.[23]

Pressure drag dominates in human swimming according to a complicated value called the **Reynolds number**. The math is not very difficult, but there are some advanced physical properties at work. To avoid going into detail, it's only important to know that physicists and engineers agree that skin friction drag comprises only about 10 percent of the resistance encountered by a swimmer. Pressure and induced drag make up another 80–90 percent, with the rest accounted for by local conditions such as wave height and frequency, and water spray. So if we're not that worried about skin friction drag, why did swimming's governing body outlaw high-tech "shark skin" outfits for Olympic swimmers? It's time to talk about swimwear, and whether the suit makes the athlete.

LIKE A STURGEON: WOULD I BE FASTER IF MY SUIT HAD SCALES?

There is a wide range of choices in swim apparel for triathletes, and what you wear in the water can have a significant impact on the first leg of your race. Wet suit or swim skin? How thick should it be? Sleeves or no sleeves? Are there any advantages to catch panels? The answers depend on how the suit interacts with your body and your aquatic medium, so we have to examine things in terms of both physics and physiology.

Wet Suits & Buoyancy

Let's first get a handle on what advantages a wet suit or swim skin gives you *in general*. A wet suit is made of neoprene, which is extremely buoyant. In other words, it displaces a large volume (and therefore mass) of water in comparison to its own mass. Therefore, in addition to its intended purpose of keeping you warm, it has the added benefit of pushing you farther out of the water and reducing the overall surface area of your body that comes in contact with the water. Furthermore, the added buoyancy around your hips and legs will lift the aft section of your body and keep you more streamlined, reducing your induced drag.

International triathlon rules state that wet suits can't be more than 5 millimeters (0.2 inches) thick. So just how much of a speed boost can 5 millimeters give you? Measurements of the body density of collegiate Division I swimmers with and without wetsuits suggest that a wetsuit only 3 millimeters thick can improve buoyancy by 2.5 percent.[24] That increased buoyancy transferred to a 3 percent reduction in time to complete a 1500-meter swim in tests on the same athletes. These findings were corroborated by another study in conditions more relevant to triathletes. It found that *a wet suit can decrease drag by about 10 percent at typical velocities for triathletes*.[25] In test conditions, triathletes made an average improvement of 6.6 percent in their 400-meter swim by using a wet suit.[26] Just as with drafting, the positive effects carried over to the cycling portion of the race, but in a much, much bigger way. When triathletes conducted a 750-meter swim at competition pace followed by a 10-minute bike at ventilatory threshold, researchers found extraordinary benefits to wet suit wear. Athletes were able to lower their stroke cadence by 14 percent, their heart rate by 11 percent, their blood lactate by 47 percent, and their cycling efficiency afterward jumped by 12 percent.[27] Thanks to a wet suit, the energy they conserved during the swim created a huge boost on the bike. These are extraordinary gains, but there's more to the story.

Wet Suit Design

Research indicates that your choice of wet suit can have a significant impact on your performance. In a study using both sleeveless and complete wet suits, dedicated swimmers experienced better results without sleeves. On the other hand, there was no discernable performance difference between the two suit types among the triathletes. The researchers concluded that swimmers rely on traveling the greatest distance possible per stroke to achieve maximum speed, and hypothesized that sleeves on a wet suit had a negative impact on their technique.[28] Meanwhile, due to their less-refined technique, the triathletes benefited equally well—or equally not-so-well, depending on how you look at it. It's just another piece of evidence that good technique is paramount to success in the water.

But racing suits have caused a lot of controversy in recent years, so much so that governing bodies were motivated to ban them from competition. Is there technology out there that can make a suit "illegally fast," and if so, just how much faster can it get?

In 2000, Speedo debuted its Fastskin swimsuit for the Olympics. Michael Phelps and other athletes famously won a record number of medals swimming in these suits. Speedo claimed that the foundation of their success was the suit's ability to reduce drag by emulating the texture of a shark's skin with special contoured ridges, called denticles. TYR quickly followed with the release of their Tracer line of swimwear, which featured ridges at specific locations along the suit to reduce drag according to the same concept. This was only the beginning of a technological battle to create the fastest possible swimwear, and the two companies were soon joined by several other manufacturers. In time, suits covered greater portions of the athletes' bodies and incorporated unique waterproof materials. World records were broken at an astonishing rate, until FINA, the governing body of international swimming, ultimately moved to ban certain technologies incorporated into suits. The Speedo LZR Racer, TYR A7, and blueseventy nero were all deemed illegal in 2010. Since then, FINA and manufacturers have continued to debate how much technology is a good thing. Textured suits are allowed, but not those made of materials deemed waterproof. Meanwhile, there are very few rules prohibiting the incorporation of such technology in Olympic triathlon, and none at all in Iron-distance events. It's fair game for those trying to gain an edge, but is there really an edge to gain?

Science says not. The claims made by suit manufacturers are founded on reducing skin friction drag. Remember from our introductory chapter that this refers to the molecules of the surrounding medium (in this case, water) clinging to the body and yanking on it as they go past. Skin friction drag makes a small contribution to the total drag of a body moving at the speed of a competitive swimmer in the water. You'd have to move much faster for it to actually make a difference. Using a special underwater apparatus that can measure the force and drag of a swimmer in a pool, scientists compared the Fastskin suit to a normal one on sixteen national-level competitive swimmers. Their results showed that the most advanced suits had no clear drag-reducing effect. They concluded that, at the top levels of Olympic competition, where hundredths of a second make the difference between gold and silver, the more advanced suits might possibly grant an athlete an edge.[29] In anything less than ideal conditions—open water competition, for instance—there's no benefit. There's an important distinction to be made at this point. In principle, a specially textured suit *could* reduce drag on a swimmer. To do so, the denticles or ridges would have to protrude 4 millimeters (0.16 inches) from the surface.[30] No suit's texture approaches that amount of difference. Instead, other unique properties gave these new suits a slight edge over older designs. Though miniscule, their benefits still counted in races where the difference between a gold medal and fourth place is often measured in hundredths of a second.

The advantage comes from the materials used to make them. They were made of nearly waterproof synthetics and crafted to the specific dimensions of the Olympians who wore them. This had two significant results. First, air bubbles became trapped around the legs and lower torso of the athletes as they put the suits on. This gave them added buoyancy that could have resulted in a small advantage. Scientists also speculated that the high amount of tension over the athletes' skin helped to reduce deformations in muscles when they weren't in a contraction phase, thus keeping a swimmer's surface more rigid as it passed through the water. Wet suits and skin suits already afford a triathlete these benefits.

In sum, a wet suit or skin suit mainly contributes to swimming performance by raising a triathlete's body out of the water and lifting her hips and legs so that the trunk is in a more streamlined position. No suit has the amount of surface area texture necessary to reduce drag, and even if it did, the effects would be minimal. *The criteria an athlete should use when choosing a wet suit are its thickness, ease of use, and flexibility.*

The swim is the shortest portion of a triathlon, but as you know from experience and now understand from a scientific standpoint, it can be the toughest. It establishes not only what position in which you start the all-important bike leg, but also your relative fatigue level as you begin pedaling. What we've seen in this chapter is that getting out of the water in the best shape possible is a matter of applying solid, fundamental concepts to increasing your efficiency in the water. The benefits you get from "advanced technologies" of various suits and devices are at best minimal and at worst highly questionable. Science strongly recommends you save your money on gimmick technologies and instead spend it on a technique clinic. Work dilligently on form in your training, then come race day focus on being a *very close* second (the closer the better when it comes to drafting!). The name of the game is efficiency. Make the best time for the least effort possible. It pays off down the road.

And speaking of down the road, let's turn our attention to the next part of our race. It's time to get on the bike!

CHAPTER 3

THE BIKE & POWER

THE BIKE IS ONE OF THE MOST DISCUSSED ASPECTS OF TRIATHLON. Whether you're talking about the instrument or the racecourse, triathletes have as many opinions about the bike as they do questions. There are good reasons for this. First, even at the elite level a triathlete spends as much of his race on the bike as swimming and running combined. This proportion holds true at every conventional race distance (sprint, Olympic, 70.3, and 140.6). Gains in bike performance therefore pay the most dividends in a triathlete's overall finishing time. Additionally, the bike becomes the most time-efficient way to improve race results because less time is wasted transitioning from one discipline to another in training.

The greater proportionate distance of the bike leg also influences financial and technological considerations for equipment, because it's on the bike where the odds of something going wrong are greatest. Obvious mechanical problems can occur, such as a tire puncture or a broken chain, but there are also strong physiological considerations. The bike begins with a transition out of a frenetic swim (oftentimes involving salt water) and ends with a second transition into a long, hard run. Sandwiched between the oxygen-deprivation of the swim and the muscular exhaustion of the run, the bike challenges triathletes to get the most they possibly can from it.

For these reasons triathletes and bike manufacturers have grown progressively more focused on the time and energy a bike and bike-related products can save an athlete. Although athletes have benefited from the innovation of several potent technologies, there has been a negative side effect. There are so many cycling-related products boasting advantages today that it's difficult for athletes to budget for their equipment. The bike budget isn't just measured in terms of dollars, either. Every added piece of aerodynamic equipment adds weight to the bike, and not all aerodynamic devices are created equal. Some provide more advantages than others. That's to say nothing of the other components that contribute to a bike's speed. In a marketplace where everything can make you faster, it becomes important to know which items make you fastest and which are of relatively marginal benefit. The good news is that science provides us with some reliable guidelines on setting our priorities.

Athletes should take encouragement that it's not hard to discriminate among most product designs. With a solid understanding of the principles at work and a little research, you can achieve greater speed and efficiency. So let's get inside the wonderful invention known as the bicycle and figure out how to get more miles per gallon of sweat!

LET'S ROLL: THE BODY & THE MEDIUM

When it comes to cycling, the body in question is the most complex of any we'll discuss because it actually consists of *two* bodies working as one: the bike and the athlete. As far as gravity and wind are concerned, you and your bike are a single, combined object. If wind pushes against you and slows you down, the bike slows down with you. And if gravity pulls the bike over and causes it to fall, you go along for the ride. You don't just transition onto

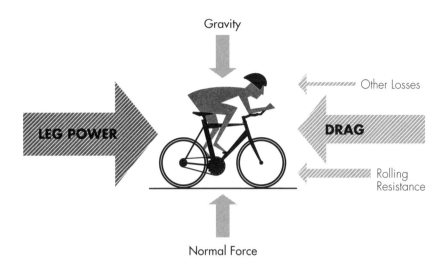

When the force the athlete generates is greater than drag, rolling resistance, and other losses, the bike will accelerate. When the athlete's force is equal to resistive forces, the bike will travel at constant speed.

the bike, you *become part* of it. It could be said that the cyclist is the original cyborg: part man, part machine, all athlete. Maybe this is the more esoteric reason triathletes fawn over their bikes so much. You share a combined mass, a center of gravity, a velocity, and a common fate on the road! With our minds open to that reality, let's check out your new body and the forces that act on it.

Gravity & Normal Force

Let's take care of the easiest stuff first. You and the bike have a combined mass. The gravitational force of the earth acts on your mass by pulling downward on it. We can measure that phenomenon either as a force in newtons or as weight in pounds. The ground under your wheels is solid enough to exert an upward force equal to gravity that keeps you from falling through the surface of the planet. We call that upward force the **normal force**.

Friction & Rolling Resistance

As we roll along, the force of gravity continues to pull downward on you, keeping your bike's tires firmly grounded on the road. The surface of the pavement and the tires' rubber interact to create friction, which keeps the bike from sliding out from underneath you or spinning out as you transfer force to them. When this interaction is favorable, we call it **traction**. But friction acts in all directions along the ground, meaning that while it keeps the bike from going directions you don't want it to, it also impedes your forward motion. Thankfully, friction is not a large enough force acting against you to be considered. Resistance from your tires comes in another form, however. As gravity pulls your mass against the earth, your tires "squish" a little against the ground, flattening out where they touch the road surface. This region between the tire and the road is known as the **contact patch**, and the technical term for "tire squishing" is **deformation**. The process of deformation constantly occurs as a new region of the tire rolls down into contact with the road. On the back side of the contact patch, the formerly deformed part of the tire must reassume its rounded shape. All this "squishing" and "unsquishing" requires energy, and the only place it can get energy is from your legs. Scientists define this energy loss as a force they call **rolling resistance**, which we see in our figure on page 43 and will discuss in the next chapter.

Drag

We saw how drag acts on your body during the swim. Drag behaves much the same way during the bike, only you are moving through air rather than water. The only real difference is that air is less dense and moves faster. We won't see wave drag on the bike, but pressure drag and skin friction drag will rear their heads again in an effort to slow us down.

Other Losses

We lump the final force acting against you into the category of "other losses." Though your body is still producing the force that drives you forward, it has to go through a few steps before it can get to the rear wheel, where it interacts with the ground. Your leg mashes on the pedal, the pedal transfers force to the crank, the crank pulls on the chain, the chain pulls on the rear cog, the cog turns the hub, the hub rotates the wheel, and then finally the wheel rolls along the ground. It works like a mechanical bucket brigade, pouring the force from your legs from one point to another until it can finally be thrown against the ground. And just like any bucket brigade, every time there's an exchange of force a slight amount gets spilled. Your bike's crank arms flex ever so slightly. There are tiny levels of friction in the joints of the chain and the ball bearings of the bottom bracket. The same goes for the bushings holding the two pulleys in the rear derailleur and the ball bearings within the hub. In addition, there's another hidden form of spillage in the tires when they flex as they roll over the road. We call this spillage in your tires and your frame **hysteresis**. Combined, these hystereses add up to drain a measurable, but not substantial, amount of power. Because of their relatively small contribution and because they act more internally on the bike than other forces do, we lump them together in the "other losses" category.

Propulsion/Power

Once again, there's only one force to battle against all the resistance: you. The size of the force you generate will determine the acceleration of your mass. We'll discuss shortly how we measure that force on the bike and why that measurement is so important.

Once you begin discussing the various points of drag and efficiency losses of the total system, things become complicated quickly. The body (bike and rider) moves through air along a paved surface, but not all paved surfaces are equal. Some roads are rougher than others. And those roads also go up and down hills of varying steepness, which modifies the impact of gravity. Gravity is the proverbial bear of cycling: Sometimes you get it, sometimes it gets you. Because we want every possible advantage, we seek out the best bike our budget can buy: light enough to beat gravity and aerodynamic enough to cheat drag.

In that regard, the advertising is true. Your choice of a bike and its components can open a doorway to success in your next race or throw up a wall for you to hit halfway through. Given an understanding of some very simple principles, you'll be rolling on the road to success.

FINDING A BETTER BODY: ALL THE FASTEST PARTS MIGHT NOT ADD UP TO SPEED

If you spend much time in bike shops or transition areas, you are likely to hear someone say, "That's a fast bike!"

Really? Is a bike sitting on the rack or in the display window actually fast? No! Its velocity is zero! A scientist would describe a bike as having low mass, or being colorful, or reflective, or more or less expensive than another bike. But she would vigorously protest that any bike at rest is fast. That bike is *stationary*! A bike without a rider is like a Ferrari without an engine. Physics holds it in place until you get on it and start pedaling. Even then the bike may not necessarily be fast. You have to apply enough force to overcome friction and air resistance to achieve a sufficiently fast velocity. That being the case, the bike will only go fast so long as your legs can work hard enough. **Of all the equipment on your bike, your legs are the most critical component.** They are the engine to your human-powered vehicle. So before you hand over the cash for those snazzy aero wheels or a superlight carbon frame, take a look in the mirror. There is no upgrade that trumps a powerful engine. There are lots of nice bikes on the road, and there are lots of athletes riding them slowly.

When it comes time to upgrade your bike, you have to take into account the impact that a single part can have on the whole. Triathlon bike frames are more aerodynamic than road bike frames, but that aerodynamic shape often comes with a penalty: They are heavier. Everything impacts everything else, and depending on what you're trying to accomplish, you may or may not get the outcome you are hoping for.

Generally, manufacturers discuss the specific component of the bike that they make: frame, wheels, handlebars, etc. Although this is perfectly understandable, marketing claims oversimplify what's really going on. A particular wheel or component may be more aerodynamic than its competitor, but that doesn't guarantee it will have a positive effect once it is bolted on to the larger bike/rider body. Aerodynamic tests show that putting all the fastest components on a fast frame may not make the fastest bike because the interactions between components are often as important as their individual properties. Some components will definitely make you faster. Some are questionable. Some are doubtful. It's similar to a bodybuilder claiming that he can pick a 500-pound weight off the ground with one arm. That's not actually what is happening. His legs and core muscles are pivotal to accomplishing the movement, and they need to be strong too. Try putting Arnold Schwarzenegger's arms on Pee-wee Herman. That 500 pounds isn't going anywhere! The whole is greater than the sum of the parts. The same philosophy is true when it comes to upgrading equipment. It's not about who chooses the most equipment or who spends the most on that equipment, it's about who selects their equipment most wisely.

Making the wise choice requires us to sharpen our "cyborg cyclist" model. You are part man, part machine, but it's not a fifty-fifty split. The rider is actually *much* more than half of the body. **The bike typically makes up 30 percent of your total aerodynamic resistance, less than 15 percent of your total bike/rider mass, and 0 percent of the power generation.**

Now look at your bike budget. How much money do you spend on stuff that makes the bike better and how much do you spend on stuff that makes *you* better? Odds are you spend a lot more on wheels, tires, and accessories than you do your engine. In fact, with all the money spent on triathlon bikes every year, few people purchase the one piece of equipment that ought to be on every bike.

THE TRIATHLETE'S SECRET WEAPON: THE BEST EQUIPMENT MONEY CAN BUY

Despite having been introduced to consumers over a decade ago and covered extensively by endurance sports web sites, magazines, and blogs, this piece of equipment has yet to become widely adopted in the sport of triathlon. It's the worst-kept secret in cycling ever to remain a secret, and it's still the best "secret weapon" available to you today. The most valuable piece of gear you could ever buy to help your cycling will definitely add a little drag and weight to your ride. It will do nothing to enhance your bike, and yet it has the potential to markedly improve your racing in no time at all. A *power meter* is the most valuable piece of gear you could ever buy for your bike.

That's pretty big talk for such a small gadget. You might be thinking, "Oh no, not a power meter! You need a degree in rocket science to use one!" Or maybe you are thinking you can't afford a power meter because you need some other accessories more. The concept of power can be intimidating to triathletes. It conjures thoughts of sophisticated transducers, expensive computers, complicated analytic software that requires a team of engineers to interpret, and a training plan written by an expensive professional coach. In fact, power is less complicated than many of the concepts in this book. As for your bike gear priorities, remember our cyborg cyclist. Man before machine, right? Next to the essential items you require to ride safely, a power meter should be the first item on a triathlete's list of indispensible speed gear. We need to upgrade the engine before adding accessories.

Regardless of whether you ride with a power meter or not, you've probably at least heard of **power** in discussions about a certain professional athlete's "wattage." What does it all mean? ***Power is defined as the rate at which energy is transferred.*** That transfer can take on many forms: electrical, chemical, and kinetic. Depending on the form power takes, we measure it in different units, but the principle is the same. Automotive enthusiasts talk about horsepower. The lightbulbs in your house are rated by the wattage they can tolerate, as are your legs and lungs. The car's engine turns the wheels; an electrical generator causes lightbulbs to glow; your legs spin the pedals. Whether it's an engine, a generator, or your legs, there is a *limit*. Send too much power into a lightbulb and it will blow. Push an engine too far past the red line and it will overheat and crack. Run an electrical generator too hard and it will melt down. It's the same with your legs. Is it any wonder that triathletes often use similar terminology to describe what happens to their bodies when they push too hard?

Every other device that uses power has a warning label or a gauge so you can make sure you're using it safely. That's what a power meter can do for your body. Why not use one, especially since your body's irreplaceable?

Before we unravel the mysteries of the watt, there's something else you need to know about power: ***The units don't matter.*** It's true! If watts have never made much sense to you, consider the following questions: Does your heart rate monitor count the beating of the lower or upper chambers of your heart? Is a marathon longer if you measure it in miles or kilometers? Would you rather have six pairs of running shoes or a half dozen? It's all the same. The units are really just a point of reference. "North" in Spanish is "Norte." Whether your map is in English or Spanish, walking that direction long enough will still get you an audience with a polar bear. The same thing goes for your legs and a power meter. Whether you measure your output in watts, horsepower, or ergs, it only matters that you are oriented to how hard your engine is working and how close it is to its limit.

Most triathletes think they wouldn't know how to use a power meter if they had one. It's easier than you think, and well worth the effort to learn.

With a little work on your part, a power meter will refine your perception of your range of power and prevent you from red-lining at the wrong time. If you're still unsure about the usefulness of power meters, there are two very good web sites that can help you.

The SRM Power Meter blog (www.srm.de) has a section dedicated to triathlon. The power output files of different professional athletes competing in races around the world reveal how *consistent* the top athletes keep their effort throughout an entire race. Regardless of wind conditions or hills, their power remains even. This shows how strong they are as athletes, but it also shows that they are very efficient in how they manage their effort. They don't let themselves burn out when the road gets steep. They're *patient*. It's difficult for an amateur triathlete to achieve this level of consistency and efficiency without feedback.

If you want to test-drive a power meter, check out Strava (www.strava .com). It is a social networking site for cyclists and runners that allows you to upload GPS data from your bike computer or smartphone and calculate certain metrics, including your power output during various stages of a ride. Strava's computer brain doesn't need you to use a power meter to give you an estimation of your output. It takes your position and speed data, along with some information about you and your bike, and uses the exact same equations given in this book to estimate your power. The calculation run by Strava's server cannot give you your exact power output, but when compared to the actual readings from a power meter, the results are quite accurate. The only drawback is that this tool helps you establish your power zones after each ride. Power is far more useful to you when you use a meter for real-time data as you ride.

There are much more sophisticated things you can do with power meters to measure and plan your training, but everything else is optional. Ultimately, a power meter defines your red line and helps you pace during a race. (See Chapter 6 for more on pacing for different race distances.) This chapter will continue to explore how the ability to monitor and regulate your power output makes you faster on the bike and puts you in position to have a much better run after you're out of the saddle. No other piece of equipment can do that for you.

But what about all the reasons *not* to buy one? After all, there are dozens of pro triathletes who don't use a power meter, power meters are expensive, and you might think that upgrading your bike is the first priority.

First, professional competitors move at speeds close to the absolute limit of our biological potential as humans.[1] A professional triathlete can get away with not using a power meter because he is competing against a small group of known individuals and his goal is clear: to be the first across the finish line. There's a small margin that separates the winner from the losers, sometimes only seconds. When this is the case, managing your power output is not necessarily as important because your effort level is defined by your competitors and the limits of what is physically possible. It is important to note how similar the average power outputs of these athletes are. When you look at their bodies, bike positions, times, and speeds, it's almost like they are the same person: a superathlete.

Compare the pro field to age groupers at your next race. You'll likely find a much more diverse range of performance among the latter. Most athletes don't come anywhere close to the absolute performance of super-athletes.[2] Furthermore, there is a much greater variety of strengths and weaknesses among age groupers. Each person's capabilities and limits are highly unique. You can't gauge your effort based on how someone else is riding. Most of us also don't spend as much time on the bike as the pros do, and we're less attuned to how our legs feel in the moment and what that means for our performance 50 miles down the road. This is why measuring power is so helpful to the amateur athlete, because it increases your awareness. It's also why we are beginning to see more professionals training and racing with power meters.

When you compare the cost of a power meter and competing upgrades, you'll see why the power meter receives the distinction of being the most valuable piece of cycling equipment you can own. Yes, power meters can be expensive. However, they are not more expensive than most of the sets of aerodynamic wheels seen on triathlon bikes. Given the choice between a new set of wheels and a power meter, skip the cosmetics and work on your engine. Get the most speed for your dollar. Remember the difference between a fast-looking bike and a bike that actually goes fast.

KNOWING WHAT'S WATT: THE FUNDAMENTALS OF POWER ON THE BIKE

Power is not exclusive to cycling. In fact, you are creating power on the swim and the run too, but it can't be as easily measured. Because of the complex movements of your arms and legs in swimming and running, scientists have yet to invent a power meter that can attach to your body without significantly hindering you in those events. However, they have measured running and swimming power with some rather large devices in laboratories and pools. Power is more easily measured on the bike because there are fixed attachment points for the power meter, either at the pedals or the hub. Furthermore, these fixed attachment points have uniform geometry and motion. Compared to the losses to water we experienced in the pool, the bike "collects" all our power output and neatly converts it.

Regardless of whether you are collecting the data or not, you are gener-ating power in everything you do. How does force relate to power, though? Part of the process is mathematical; part is conceptual. You apply a force against the pedal of your bike. The crank begins to move and so does the bike. The force causes the bike, which has mass, to accelerate. That fits in with Newton's second law:

$$F = ma$$

That is, force equals mass times acceleration. So if force causes the bike to move, where did power occur? It takes another step to get there. After we get the bike to our desired speed, we continue to pedal at a steady rate.

That means there's no acceleration. According to the equation, it might at first seem that there's no force. But remember that it's the *sum* of the forces that equals zero acceleration. You still have to pedal to maintain a constant speed, which means you're constantly overcoming forces working against you. That makes sense, because we know that our medium involves resistance from the road and the air. The force with which you pedal equals the forces opposing you. These forces are changing constantly, and as a result the force you exert on the pedals varies greatly with each turn of the cranks.

Measuring the force your legs produce throughout each revolution of an entire workout would be the most direct way to analyze your endurance and effort management. However, there are significant complications with this method. Because different muscles engage as the crank arms turn, the force on the pedals is constantly in flux. Scientists have broken the crank revolution into four distinct regions according to the amount of force a person applies to the pedal through them, and there are thousands of crank revolutions in an average ride, so it's difficult to collect or assess the data in a meaningful way. It would also be futile to expect athletes to keep their eyes glued to the computer to keep things constant. What we need is a way to average things out. Although the amount of force bounces all over the place with each turn of the pedals, measuring it over distance gives us a way to provide readings over a more gradual and easily interpreted range. If we pedal our bike 5, 10, or 20 miles, we can develop a metric to assess our effort over that period and change the readout so that it's manageable. We call that metric **work**, and it is represented by the letter W.

$W = Fd$

*Where **W** is work, **F** is force, and **d** is distance.*

Once again, keep in mind the units are not important. That's especially true for work because it is an in-between step on the way to calculating power. We actually could have skipped this step, but it's good to see it here because you might see it more frequently if you decide to measure your power. Computer applications that track power will often provide a summary of your ride that includes total work, which is measured in kilojoules, or kJ for short. The unit for work is known as the joule. It is sometimes also referred to as a newton-meter, which simply refers to the product of force and distance. Work requires us to compare our effort over a distance. As athletes, we're more used to measuring against the clock. It would make things more intuitive if we could measure our effort against time. Just one more step to go!

Let's consider for a moment what our equation for work tells us. What if we're about to race on a 112-mile bike course? Our distance suddenly becomes fixed in the equation, leaving only a direct relationship between force and work. Pedal harder, and we'll do more work. Pedal easier, and we'll do less. Something else changes when we increase or decrease our effort: the time it takes us to complete the distance. Apply more force and you do more work, but you'll do it in less time. This is all fine and good if we're pedaling a fixie, but it's more fun to shift gears to maintain our speed. We've all noticed before that we can actually go *faster* by pedaling easier—we just have to turn the cranks faster. That puts an extra twist on our problem. How do we account for it? Simple. We apply less force to the pedal each time we push on it when we shift into an easier gear, but because the cranks are turning faster, we wind up applying that force several more times over a given distance than we would in a bigger gear. Think of it this way:

$$1 + 1 + 1 + 1 + 1 + 1 = 6$$

$$2 + 2 + 2 = 6$$

If you push a gear that's twice as big, you only have to push it half as many times, but you have to push it twice as hard. There are all kinds of ways to get things to add up to six—you just have to decide which works best for you.

We can conclude that there's a relationship between how hard we work and the rate at which the work is completed. Congratulations, you've just discovered power.

$$P = \frac{W}{t}$$

*Where **P** is power, **W** is work, and **t** is time.*

We know the unit for power is the watt. One watt equals one joule per second. That doesn't really mean much to us as athletes, and therein lies the problem. When a manufacturer claims a particular product design shaves off so many grams, thereby reducing drag and saving us some precious watts, how can we tell if the product will really boost performance?

Remember that the concept of wattage is related to force. So if an athlete could reduce the magnitude of the forces opposing him, then he could reduce the amount of power required to achieve a certain speed. Shave a few grams off your bike and you don't have to produce as much power to overcome the force of gravity pulling you backwards on a tough hill. Reduce your air resistance and you don't need as many watts to hit 25 mph on a flat straightaway. This is the philosophy behind every advertisement for products and methods claiming to save precious watts. The ultimate question is, just how precious is a watt?

WHAT'S IT WORTH?: THE RELATIVE VALUE OF A WATT

We know that a watt is equal to one joule per second, and we know that a joule is equal to a force of one newton exerted over a distance of one meter. The problem is that you can have all this information and still not know anything. What does a watt *feel* like? Here's a basis for comparison: The top professional men competing in an Ironman race will average anywhere between 270 and 320 watts over the 112 miles of the bike course. They will generate as much as 600 watts in short bursts, depending on wind conditions and the terrain. Professional women average between 180 and 220 watts over the entire course, with short bursts upward of 400 watts. This amounts to a 4.5-hour effort for the men, and about 5 hours for the women. An extremely good amateur male athlete can probably average between 220 and 260 watts for 112 miles. Now let's consider the average triathlete.

Hypothetically, let's say our average triathlete is a thirty-something writer who has to fit his training in between giving interviews, paying bills, going to baseball games with his son, and finishing a really great book about the science of triathlon. He rides his bike on a stationary trainer for an hour three to four times a week and gets a two- to four-hour ride in on the weekends. It's possible that an athlete like that could produce 260 watts . . . *for an hour*. After that, his output level would likely drop precipitously. If he needed to ride 112 miles at a consistent output and then run a marathon, he'd probably have to pull the throttle back to about 200 watts. If he didn't, it's possible he'd find himself averaging about 220 watts for the first 50 miles and only about 160 watts for the last 40 miles, and then cursing himself for a fool as he left T2. In such a case, our hypothetical athlete would probably mutter to himself throughout the entire marathon that he knew better than to go out too hard and that he should have heeded the warnings of his power meter. Thank goodness this is only a hypothetical situation, and that no real athlete ever had to suffer such a humiliating race result in order to prove this simple fact: **No gadget or piece of equipment can help you if you don't use it wisely.**

So just how much of a wattage savings is significant? At this point we get into something of a numbers game dealing with scientific error. Since the average athlete's power output will range anywhere between 150 and 250 watts in a race, it seems like every single watt counts. After all, a watt here, a watt there, pretty soon you've got some serious power! The problem is that a single watt will always be a measurement so small that it exists within the range of statistical error. In other words, if scientists were measuring the power output of two different cyclists and one produced 1 watt more or less than the other one, then they would say that the two cyclists produced an equal amount of power. This is actually good news for triathletes who don't want to obsess over numbers or get too detailed in how they use their power meter, because in many ways your relationship with a power meter works like the relationship you have with your heart rate monitor. No one goes out on a run to maintain a perfect 164 beats per minute throughout the workout. That's impossible. You don't have that much control over your body. Instead, coaches and athletes track their performance by staying in distinct heart rate zones. It should be no surprise then that the same concept applies to power. Furthermore, power zones have been devised into the same categories as heart rate training zones: recovery, endurance, tempo, threshold, etc. That's exactly why you don't need to read an entire textbook to use a power meter. After riding with one for about two weeks, you'll quickly figure out what your zones are by your own intuition. That sense of things will improve with time, and during your races you'll know if you're pedaling too hard for your own good. On the gear side of the issue, there are too many variables in experimental conditions for scientists to rule out the possibility that their instruments aren't calibrated correctly or that one of the test subjects was just having a bad day. Depending on the test conditions, what the researchers are looking for, and the sensitivity of the equipment, scientists probably need 5 to 8 watts of difference in order to call it significant. That doesn't tell us how precious the difference is, but it's a good rule of thumb.

In fact, there's an even more useful rule of thumb that product manufacturers use for evaluating performance: *10 watts will save approximately 40 to 60 seconds over a distance of 25 miles.*[3]

The 10-watt threshold gives us a very good measuring stick to use whenever we consider a new equipment purchase or evaluate our training. Any gain or loss of fewer than 5 watts is negligible because in the greater scheme of things, we can't be certain a specific item is solely responsible for the change. If your power meter says your maximum output during a test session was 5 watts fewer than previously, it doesn't necessarily mean you've gotten weaker. Likewise, any piece of equipment that only saves 5 watts may or may not actually grant you any benefits. Two hundred watts would grant us some staggering benefits. However, there isn't a single bike or tactic out there that's going to save us that much power in one fell swoop. The trick is to figure out where the most power savings can be made, compare that to the dollars you have to spend to achieve those power savings, and then get the right combination to maximize the gains from your bike budget.

As we begin our search for the optimal approach, we immediately come to a fork in the road. Looking at our medium, we see there are two primary forces acting against us: gravity and air resistance. Is it better to have a lighter bike or a more aerodynamic one, and why?

CHAPTER 4

THE BIKE: WEIGHT & AERODYNAMICS

THERE'S A DIFFERENCE BETWEEN A WISE DECISION and a decision made wisely. Given a choice between two options, even a coin flip stands a fifty-fifty chance of "getting it right." The answer may be correct, but there's nothing wise about the method.

Triathletes invest too much time and money—not to mention blood, sweat, and tears—and value their results too highly to leave their choices about bike equipment to chance, advertising hype, or peer pressure. The bike industry boasts a tremendous number of breakthroughs and advancements in cycling technology every year. The wise athlete discriminates between these developments according to their relative value. Although your racing and training goals are personal and unique to you, the principles of physics give all athletes a perspective on what matters most. They may not always lead you to make the right decision, but they will increase your odds of doing so.

CLIMBERS BEWARE: WORKING AGAINST THE WEIGHT OF THE WORLD

Most triathletes follow a pretty standard pattern of bike shopping. They see a really "fast bike" (that you now know isn't actually fast!) sitting in the store, walk over to it, and pick it up. They'll heft it a couple of times and remark how light it is. They do the same thing with wheels, handlebars, saddles, and anything else they can pick up. Shop owners and customers say the same thing to each other all the time: "Oh! Feel how light that is!" Once again, our savvy scientist becomes agitated. You cannot measure how light something is. You measure its mass and the relative influence gravity has on it. The next time you find yourself lifting things in a shop, make sure you exclaim to everyone around you how impressively heavy the bikes are.

Joking aside, we see once again that our misconceptions about physics often come with penalties. We can find bikes and components that have relatively more or less mass than others, but both the bike and the rider have mass, and gravity will pull down on them. It is not only an inescapable situation, but a necessary one. That we don't fully appreciate this aspect of cycling and constantly seek to "cut weight" calls into question whether we're doing the right thing. We already know that reducing mass is a "body" modification that is less beneficial than upgrading our motor, but if we are already working on upgrading our legs through training, a little improvement to the bike itself can't hurt. The question is how much it can help. Understanding those relative benefits depends on getting better acquainted with gravity and how the scales tip in our favor (or against it!) as the roads pitch up and down.

At the top of page 61 we have our typical case: a bike moving along a flat and level surface. Gravity holds it firmly against the road and off it goes. The only way gravity serves to oppose the bike's forward movement is through rolling resistance in the wheel, according to the equation for rolling resistance, which we'll discuss in more detail later. Things change when the bike begins to move uphill.

Gravity
Normal Force
Rolling Resistance

In the figure below, things get more difficult. Gravity still acts in the same direction, but because the bike has changed its orientation, gravity's effect on it has changed. The gravitational force is now broken into two components. The first component still holds you down on the ground. Notice, however, that this component is slightly less than the gravitational force was when the bike was on level ground. That portion of gravitational force is not lost. Instead it contributes to the second component, which begins to act against your direction of movement. A certain proportion of

Gravity
Normal Force
Rolling Resistance

our power generation must now overcome the downward force of gravity. We're all instinctively aware that the steeper the hill, the more difficult it gets. That's because our effort increasingly works in opposition to gravity. So as the road grade increases, it becomes more difficult to move because a greater portion of gravity acts in direct opposition to our direction of travel. It would be nice if there were a way to figure out exactly what the relationship is. As it turns out, there is. Look out: Here comes trigonometry! Don't worry, this is going to make things much simpler.

Let's take things step by step. First, look at the figure below showing hills of increasing steepness, or grade. We start with a small angle of 20 degrees and increase to 45 and then 60 degrees. It's obvious which incline would be most difficult to climb. The angles are exaggerated here to better illustrate the concept.

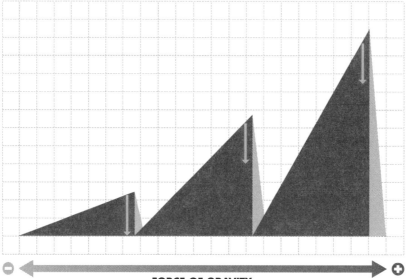

FORCE OF GRAVITY

It's worth noting just how large a difference a small change in angle can make in the real world, though. Whenever a highway maintains a grade of 6 percent or greater for a mile or more, there will be signs warning drivers of steep grades. When the grade increases, all but the fittest (or most stubborn) climbers will decide that discretion and the small chainring are the better part of valor and gear down. An 8-degree angle doesn't seem like much at all—you'd be upset if someone cut you a slice of pizza with that measurement! But look what 8 degrees correspond to on a bike. A 14 percent grade is a monster. All that worry and lactic acid over 8 little degrees? Indeed. Gravity is undeniably a force to be reckoned with. Observe the following angles and their corresponding grades. They redefine our concept of "six degrees of separation."

ANGLE	ROAD GRADE
4°	7%
5°	8.75%
6°	10.5%
7°	12.3%
8°	14%
9°	16%
10°	17.5%

Armed with that understanding, let's return to our ridiculously steep climb to get an idea of what's happening with gravity when we start going up. First, let's think of our situation in the context of two scenarios: pedaling your bike on a flat road and straight up a wall. When on the flats, gravity acts perpendicular to your direction of motion, so it doesn't do anything to directly oppose you. On the other hand, if you try to pedal straight up a wall, you won't get anywhere. If you think you can't get up the wall because gravity pulls down on you so hard, you're only half right. Not only is gravity working hard against you, it's not doing any work *for* you either. This is where friction factors in. When you're going down a flat road, gravity holds your tires to the surface and gives you traction. When you go straight up, gravity is *parallel* to your motion, and so your traction is zero. It actually wouldn't matter if there were any force pulling against you or not. Your tires would just spin out unless they were magnetically attached to the wall. What this means is that as we transition from a flat road to an impossibly upright one, gravity works in some combination of a perpendicular and parallel force. These are the components of the gravitational force, and you can see how they add up to equal the total gravitational force in the figure below.

Regardless of the bicycle's direction of travel, the forces acting on it must always be resolved into how they work according to the bike's frame of reference: forward, backward, up, down, and side-to-side. Breaking the gravitational force into components allows us to see it in those essential directions. Now our only challenge is to figure out what those force components equal. The triangle formed by the gravitational force and its two components matches nicely with the angle of the hill, as we see below.

This relationship between the angles allows us to come up with some equations that define the force of gravity acting against us as the angle of the climb increases. It doesn't matter what angle we're dealing with, the relationships are always the same.

MEASURING GRAVITATIONAL FORCE

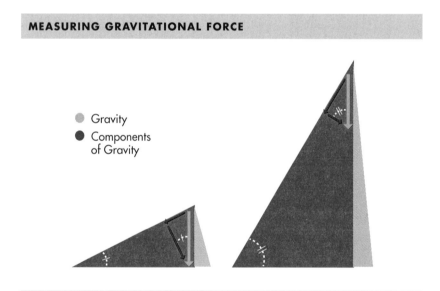

Gravity always acts downward, but the components of the gravitational force always act parallel and perpendicular to the athlete's direction of motion. A hill's angle of incline changes the athlete's direction of motion relative to gravity, and thus the magnitude of the gravitational components.

The force acting against you when you climb can be calculated with the following equation:

$$F = mg \times sin(\theta)$$

*Where **F** is the force of gravity pulling you backward, **m** is the total mass of bike and rider, **g** is the force of gravity (9.81 m/s²), and **θ** is the angle of the incline.*

Now that we have the equation to calculate the force pulling back against you, we can use it to determine the required power to maintain speed going up a hill based on the steepness of the hill. Let's assume we have a 150-pound triathlete riding a 15-pound bike up a hill at three different speeds, as shown on page 66. How hard does he have to work to hold his pace?

It would be quite hard for our hypothetical triathlete to maintain a speed of 20 mph at anything more than a 3 percent road grade. His power output would be approaching 300 watts before the hill even begins to feel steep! This illustrates how a power meter can help recreational athletes. That hill might not feel so tough when you're just starting out, but adrenaline and fresh legs have a habit of suckering you into pushing way too hard. You don't realize it until you hit a similar hill late in the day. By then it's too late. If you have a power meter and have refined your perception of your range of power, you can avoid that fate.

Returning to the graph on page 66, if our triathlete's aerobic capacity is high, he might do better than 10 mph on pitches steeper than 6 percent, but he'll have to pump out more than 400 watts to keep going at 20 mph up steep hills. He might be able to do that for a half a mile or so, but if the hill stretches for several miles he's going to tire out.

There's another important point to make here. This graph assumes that our theoretical triathlete rides in a vacuum, without air resistance. That's unrealistic, but it's important to isolate the influence of gravity and mass so we can see their influence clearly. As air resistance increases, so

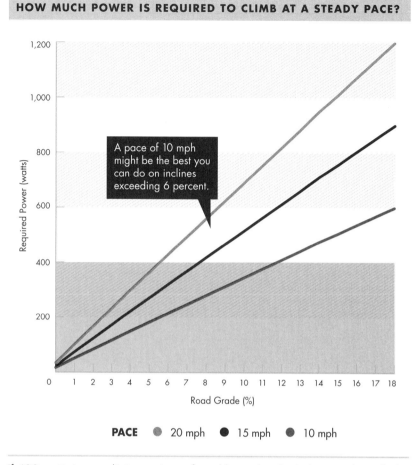

If 400 watts is a realistic maximum for athletes, the shaded region bounds the realm of mortal possibility, and everything above it verges on superhuman.

does the power required to work against it. For that reason, our graph actually underestimates the required power.

A note on weight: If you were to lose weight through proper training, your weight loss would have a dual impact on power and speed. As weight decreases, the amount of power required to maintain a certain speed will also decrease. At the same time, the amount of power you are capable of generating should actually increase. This is because oxygen uptake is related to body mass and improves as fat is lost. But we'll leave those discussions to a coach or physiologist, and take a closer look at the bike.

A WEIGHTY MATTER: THE (RELATIVE) BENEFIT OF LIGHTENING YOUR LOAD

Now that we know just how much harder life can get in the span of a few degrees of incline, it may seem more important than ever to dump any and all extra mass we can from our bikes. Yet we still need to qualify things. There's always the allure of a carbon fiber bottle cage, an upgrade to carbon fiber cranks, handlebars, stem, carbon saddle rails, or wheel spokes. Five grams here, 10 grams there, it all adds up, right? Pretty soon, you're 500 grams lighter. That's half a kilogram!

True. But such upgrades could easily total $500 or more, which is also half a *grand*. Is it worth it?

Not exactly. Let's get a little perspective on the difference between the bike leg of some of triathlon's more popular courses and the crown jewels in professional cycling. When you survey the lay of the land, you find some interesting contrasts in the approach to Ironman and UCI-style cycling.[1]

It's easy to see what makes the climbs of cycling's Grand Tours so legendary. The score is a bit more even between the tougher Ironman bike courses and the famous Spring Classics (Paris-Roubaix). Even then, professional cyclists are clamoring for the lightest equipment available. Meanwhile, triathletes are similarly fixated on aerodynamics, which often cost them when it comes to weight. Are we wrong to take a weight penalty in order to have a more aerodynamic bike? Absolutely not. There's one advantage that Pro Tour cyclists have that is typically illegal in long-distance triathlon: drafting. Because cyclists ride in a pack and take turns pulling at the front, they enjoy significant reduction in their aerodynamic resistance. You can see this concept at work in just about any stage of a professional cycling race. A small

WHY DOES WEIGHT MATTER SO MUCH TO CYCLISTS? (AND WHY DO TRIATHLETES OBSESS OVER AERODYNAMICS?)

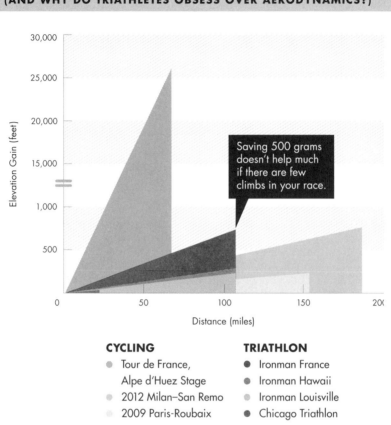

CYCLING
- Tour de France, Alpe d'Huez Stage
- 2012 Milan–San Remo
- 2009 Paris-Roubaix

TRIATHLON
- Ironman France
- Ironman Hawaii
- Ironman Louisville
- Chicago Triathlon

Weight is much more important in cycling than in triathlon because it emphasizes climbing to a much greater extent.

group typically breaks away to establish a lead of several minutes, but they are almost always caught by the main group before getting to the finish line. This happens because the breakaway consists of four to ten cyclists who have to repeatedly take turns leading without much of a break, while the peloton has a legion of riders who can take shorter turns and therefore maintain a faster pace. We'll go more in-depth on that matter shortly, but for now we'll leave it at this: The style of courses and nature of professional cycling require Pro Tour riders to be more concerned with weight than triathletes.

Just how concerned you should be about weight as a triathlete is an issue of relative importance. We have done the math and confirmed that gravity *does* exert a significant force on us. The question is whether we can really do anything about it. We know that we can't cut all of our mass, and that some of it is necessary to make the bike move in the first place. How much mass can we lose, and is it enough to be helpful? Let's examine just how much weight you can save by making the leap from aluminum to carbon on several standard components. And just for good measure, let's exchange a second-tier group set for a top-of-the-line model. Note that this analysis measures grams, not ounces or pounds, not only because the gram is the standard measurement in the endurance sports industry, but also

MASS: MID-GRADE VS. TOP-END COMPONENTS

ITEM	MASS	MASS
Trek Equinox Frame	1,908 g	1,543 g
	(7 model, aluminum)[2]	(TTX 9.0 model, carbon)[3]
Fork	650 g	550 g
Handlebars	270 g	185 g
Stem	165 g	150 g
Bottle Cages	60 g	20 g
Saddle	180 g	150 g
Bontrager Wheels[4]	1,910 g	1,320 g
	(Race)	(Race XXX Lite)
SRAM Group Set	2,441 g	2,206 g
	(Red)[5]	(Force)[6]
TOTAL MASS	7,584 G	6,124 G
MASS SAVINGS		1,460 G

because the gram is a measurement of mass, not weight. We'll use mass later on to calculate the resultant forces.

Again, it's important to *measure* in terms of mass, but just to provide some perspective, let's look at the conversion to weight (1 kilogram is equal to 2.2 pounds). With this information in hand, we can compare our two hypothetical bikes:

1,460 g × 2.2 = 3.21 lbs. total weight saved

A good approximate difference between an entry-level aluminum triathlon bike with a decent set of components and a top-of-the-line carbon model with some of the lightest components on the market is just shy of 3.25 pounds. This may just be the same amount of weight subtracted from your wallet after you've purchased the "necessary" equipment. It becomes more problematic when you consider the ways in which you spend money to *add* weight to your bike. Your "extra value meal" is costing you more than you think!

Was the weight loss worth it? Let's take our hypothetical triathlete back to our variable-incline hill and have him ride two bikes up it at the same speed (see page 71). The first bike will be the 15-pounder from our original test, and the second one will shave off the 3.21 pounds we estimated. For each test, we'll have him ride at 15 mph. Everything is constant, except for the bike, so what we ought to see is a reduction in the power requirement. That's the real test of your savings.

If you're having trouble telling what the difference is, save yourself the eyestrain. That's the message. Remember that we said in Chapter 3 (see page 57) that our rule of thumb requires a 10-watt difference before we can really consider the power difference an advantage. The difference in power output between the heavier and the lighter bike doesn't cross that threshold until the hill reaches a 10 percent grade. That is tremendously steep, and rarely seen on a triathlon course. And truth be told, the lighter bike didn't save much power at all at that grade! The argument can be made that pro athletes use the lightest equipment they can, so there must be *something* to

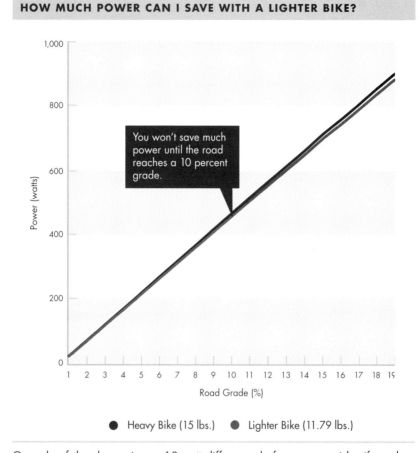

Heavy Bike (15 lbs.) ● Lighter Bike (11.79 lbs.)

Our rule of thumb requires a 10-watt difference before we can identify a clear advantage. The lighter bike doesn't cross that threshold until the climbs are tremendously steep, which is rarely seen on a triathlon course.

it. But once again you have to remember that professional athletes operate in an entirely different environment than the rest of us. They are all very close to each other in terms of fitness, and they are also all very close to being the absolute best a human being can be. The Tour de France is a 3,000-mile race that lasts nearly a month, and the difference between first and second place is typically less than a minute. At the pro cyclist level, seconds count and grams make the difference. But the majority of triathletes simply aren't at that level.

Beyond that, our result also makes intuitive sense: 3.21 pounds is just over 2 percent of the total weight of our 150-pound cyclist and 15-pound bike. Ten watts is 2 percent of the 500-watt power requirement to maintain speed up a 10 percent grade. Because the weight-to-power savings ratio is linear, we should expect that one-to-one relationship. The implication is a bitter pill, though. If you want to reduce the power requirement by 1 percent, you have to reduce the total mass of the body by 1 percent. And because our body is the triathlete and the bike *put together*, a measly 1 percent equates to a whole lot of grams before you see returns on your carbon investment!

Remember that the athlete becomes part of the body before it begins moving forward and that he holds most of the weight. Professional triathletes and cyclists maintain single-digit body fat percentages even in the off-season. It's not unusual for them to hover in the 4–12 percent range during competition, depending on gender. This has notable implications. For the athlete, it's not absolute weight that matters so much. The taller male triathletes weigh upward of 160 pounds, whereas a Tour de France champion may barely tip the scale at 140 pounds. However, because of the cyclist's training and discipline, his body is highly developed for the sport. He has lots of muscle to generate power, and no extra weight (fat or "extra muscle") holding him back. This means he has a very high **power-to-weight ratio**. Two pounds of fat equals just a little more than 900 grams. *Scientifically and economically speaking, the most effective way to shave weight off the bike is not to spend hundreds on carbon, but to avoid the extra-value meals at your local fast-food joint.*

If the power argument doesn't quite satisfy you, we can look at it another way. Let's answer the question you really care about: *How much faster does it make me?* After all, you win races by saving time, not watts. Let's see what will happen when the same triathlete rides bikes of varying weight up different hills. We'll hold power at a constant 200 watts and have him ride up a 1-mile climb at seven different grades (1–7 percent). The only other thing we'll change is the mass of the bike frame. To make this as intuitive as possible, we'll relax our rigorous scientific definitions and compare bikes in terms of weight. Let's look at the difference between 15-, 16-, 17-, and 18-pound bikes, with the 18-pound bike serving as the baseline. Because of the complexity involved, we'll eliminate air resistance and analyze the impact of weight reduction only. How much time do we save?

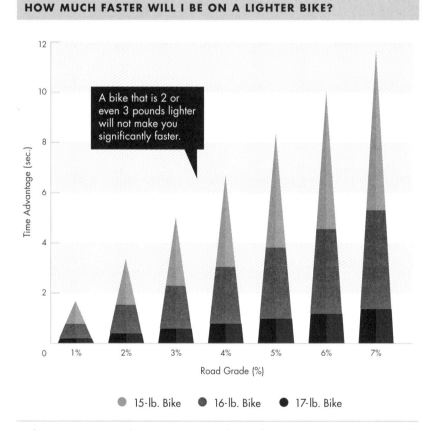

HOW MUCH FASTER WILL I BE ON A LIGHTER BIKE?

A bike that is 2 or even 3 pounds lighter will not make you significantly faster.

Time Advantage (sec.)

Road Grade (%)

● 15-lb. Bike ● 16-lb. Bike ● 17-lb. Bike

In this scenario a cyclist attempts a 1-mile climb at various road grades with progressively lighter bikes. Power is held constant at 200 watts and air resistance is not factored in. The 18-pound bike is the baseline.

Read it and weep, weight watchers. Look at the far right of the graph on page 73. Take 3 pounds off your bike, pedal at a constant rate of 200 watts, and you'll get to the top of a 7 percent climb a whole 7.5 seconds ahead of the competition. A 1-pound advantage only puts you ahead by 2.5 seconds. This makes sense when you remember the rule of thumb from our introduction to power in Chapter 3: 10 watts only saves 40–60 seconds over a distance of 25 miles. Keep in mind that the advantage only holds when the climbs are long and steep. Courses with fewer and shorter ascents will keep the difference small. Of course, this only accounts for half the situation. What goes up must come down. So how does mass influence descents in cycling?

MASS EFFECT: THE UPS & DOWNS OF BEING HEAVIER ON DESCENTS

There's one last item to take into account, and the question comes up quite frequently even among professional athletes. If weight makes it difficult to get up a hill, shouldn't it make it just as easy to go down? The heavier bike would descend faster, right? It seems pretty intuitive: If gravity acting on two objects is the same and one has more mass than the other, then Newton's second law demands that more force acts on the object with greater mass. It's a perfect application of the lessons you've already learned!

Sort of.

First, let's qualify what we know. Some people with a background in physics will actually reject this claim, and they'll have a pretty convincing argument in the findings of one of the giants of scientific history: Galileo Galilei. Galileo died in the same year Isaac Newton was born, and his discoveries—some of the greatest in history—contributed significantly to Newton's work. One of Galileo's most legendary revelations occurred during what is known as the ball drop experiment. People like to tell the story of how he walked to the top of the Leaning Tower of Pisa with two equal-sized balls of different mass and dropped them from the top of the tower while his assistant below observed that they hit the ground at the same time. This proved **Galileo's theory of falling bodies, which states that all freely falling objects accelerate at the same rate**. This theory was later proven true by Apollo astronauts on the moon when they dropped a hammer and a feather from an equal height. The two objects landed simultaneously. So if a heavier cyclist descending a hill gets to the bottom before a lighter cyclist, does that mean he defies Galileo's theory?

Not at all, as a matter of fact.

To begin, let's clear up some of the widely held misconceptions about Galileo's experiment. To begin with, the ball drop didn't take place at the Leaning Tower of Pisa. As a disciplined scientist, Galileo knew that an experiment's results have to be replicated several times before they can be accepted as true. Because he was more interested in repeating his experiment than running hill repeats, he decided to avoid climbing up and down stairs all day. Instead, he constructed a ramp and rolled the balls down it over and over, recording the amount of time they took to reach the bottom. This was how he arrived at his conclusions, and it sounds a lot like two cyclists lining up against each other for a gravity-powered drag race.

Besides getting the details right, there's a conceptual problem with our understanding of Galileo's experiment. Most people incorrectly remark that his theory states "all objects fall at the same rate, regardless of mass." But remember, Galileo said, "All freely falling objects accelerate equally." *Falling* and *falling freely* are two very different things. Free fall is a condition in which only gravity acts on the object as it falls. On earth, we are forced to deal with aerodynamic forces as we fall through a molecule-filled atmosphere. Galileo ignored air resistance in his theory. That's why the feather and hammer contest is a tie on the moon and not on earth. There's no air resistance on the moon, so all gravity-based races there are ties. The same would go for the two cyclists. But on earth, air resistance works against the less massive cyclist. The two cyclists and bikes of more or less equal size will encounter the same amount of air resistance. The force of wind against them will be a function of their respective velocities. But the heavier cyclist will have a greater force of gravity pulling him down and he'll go faster.

But as with most things in physics, there's a catch, and our debate about making your bike lighter for a triathlon isn't over. To begin with, just about everyone pedals when going down a gradual hill, and the power they apply will have a much greater influence on the race than their weight. (There's also the issue of handling, and even a modest degree of technical skill can negate a nominal weight advantage.) But even if our cyclists were of equal ability and applied the same amount of power, physics still favors the lighter competitor over the full distance of a race.

Let's put the principle to a quick illustrative test. Assume we have two athletes of equal size and shape approaching a hill. The hill goes up at a 5 percent grade for a mile, crests, and then descends at a 5 percent grade for a mile. Our athletes weigh 154 pounds (70 kg) and 130 pounds (59 kg) and produce the same amount of power, which we'll set at a gentle 150 watts. Since we haven't gone through a detailed explanation of how air resistance works yet, we'll forego a step-by-step equation and cut straight to why the lightweight cyclist gets to the bottom first. She gets up the hill with a 50-second advantage over her counterpart, which puts her about 225 meters in front. Once she gets to the top, she lets off the pedals and coasts to the bottom. Our more massive athlete does the same and . . . never catches her. Once the downhill portion begins, the heavier competitor makes up only 10 seconds and 115 meters on the lighter competitor. So what happened?

It turns out that our final discussion of mass on the bike is also our introduction to aerodynamics. As we're about to see in greater detail, air resistance quickly becomes a huge factor once we start getting up to speed. The faster you go, the harder the air pushes against you, until finally our two athletes reach a point at which the aerodynamic force pushing against them is equal to the force of gravity pulling them downhill. Based on what we've learned about Newton's Laws, we know that when the opposing forces cancel each other out, there's no more acceleration. They're going as fast as physics will allow them, a condition known as **terminal velocity**. By plotting their velocity over time and including air resistance, we see how quickly they hit terminal velocity and how little ground our heavier cyclist is able to make up.

That's a difference in athletes, though. What about weight savings on the bicycle? Well, if you cut 1,000 grams (2.2 pounds) from your bike, you'll be 5 seconds faster going up and only half a second slower going down. At the very top levels of the sport, and on certain courses, that can be a useful advantage. At the Tour de France, Andy Schleck flies up L'Alpe d'Huez

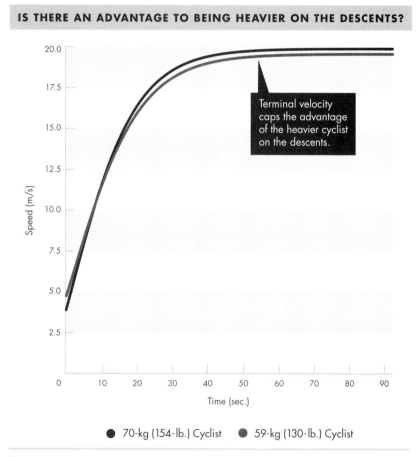

IS THERE AN ADVANTAGE TO BEING HEAVIER ON THE DESCENTS?

Terminal velocity caps the advantage of the heavier cyclist on the descents.

● 70-kg (154-lb.) Cyclist   ● 59-kg (130-lb.) Cyclist

The heavier cyclist makes up 10 seconds (115 meters), but never overcomes the 50-second (225-meter) advantage the lighter cyclist had going into the descent.

faster than 20 mph. At his speed, less than half a percent savings in mass amounts to nearly 7 watts, which can be the difference between winning and losing by a large margin in that race. But the average age-grouper triathlete rarely encounters climbs that severe outside of the Alpe d'Huez Triathlon and Ironman France. Normally, the hills in triathlon races are short and brief. Even then, the fastest age groupers at Ironman Florida and Ironman Arizona, two of the flattest courses in the entire race series, never exceed an average speed of 19.5 mph.[7] By comparison, the hilly phases of Ironman Wisconsin drop contestants down to about 10 mph.[8] Until your engine can push you over those hills faster than 15 mph, there's really no way to justify the expense involved in shedding mere grams for such a small portion of the course.

That leads us to where we *should* invest those speed dollars. It's common knowledge these days that it's all about the aero. After all, it's not for comfort that a triathlete gets into an aerodynamic position. But aerodynamics is a pretty big field of study, and there are a lot of ways to empty your wallet on aerodynamic extras. What's the best way to sow your racing budget in order to reap the biggest time gains? It's pretty simple if you know a few things. Let's shoot the breeze for a while about every triathlete's favorite subject.

AERO HEAD: THE SMART WAY TO GET FAST

"Get aero." It's the constant refrain of every triathlete. Everyone wants to be more aerodynamic, and every bike-related product advertises it can give you an aero edge. Why do we continually emphasize the aerodynamic component of cycling? What does it actually mean to be aerodynamic, and what's the best way to optimize our aerodynamics on the bike? Is there even such a thing as an optimum aerodynamic setup in the first place?

These are complicated questions, and the answers aren't always clear-cut. How air moves over an object at a given speed—whether it be a triathlete on a bike moving at 20 mph or a space shuttle breaking the sound barrier—is a chaotic and sophisticated problem that engineers constantly study. We learn new things about aerodynamics all the time. The biggest changes in bicycle technology from year to year are derived from new discoveries and developments.

That constant evolution makes it even more difficult for athletes to make decisions about what equipment will help them the most. Yesterday's fastest bike or helmet may be among the slowest today. But every competitor with a budget is asking just *how* much faster these products are, and how to get the most value for the money. There is good news, however: Although products change over time, the fundamental principles that govern the behavior of airflow and how it affects the overall performance of the bike and rider remain the same.

First, let's become more familiar with how the air behaves, because there's something significant about the way it treats all objects acting against it. Air resistance is not a constant force. ***Aerodynamic resistance against a cyclist increases exponentially with speed.***

The graph on page 80 illustrates the amount of power required for an average cyclist to maintain a given speed when faced with increasing air resistance. We can see that as he gets faster, he needs more power—*lots* more power. It's obvious just what we're up against, but the math is simple enough too. The amount of power required to accelerate a bike is proportionate to the cube of your current velocity. In other words, if you want to double your speed, you have to put out *eight times* as much power.

$$P \approx v^3$$

*Where **P** is power and **v** is velocity (distance over time).*

This is a radically different relationship from the one we observed between mass and speed when cycling uphill, and underscores the fundamental reason triathletes value aerodynamics over weight.

If this seems familiar from what we covered in Chapter 2, that is because air behaves much like water, and just as we have to fight against water resistance when we swim, we must battle our way against air resistance to make it to the end of the bike leg. The important difference for triathletes as it pertains to the bike is gear. Although no one has yet to figure out a way to make (legal) swim gear that actually assists your performance, the story is different for the bike. In fact, there are several opportunities to change a

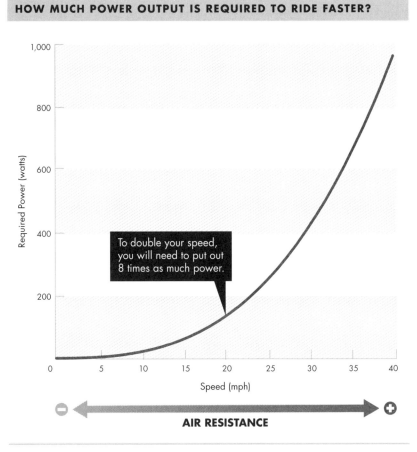

HOW MUCH POWER OUTPUT IS REQUIRED TO RIDE FASTER?

Required Power (watts)

To double your speed, you will need to put out 8 times as much power.

Speed (mph)

AIR RESISTANCE

Power to overcome air resistance increases exponentially with speed. A cyclist only needs 21 watts to move at 10 mph, but requires 171 watts at 20 mph.

cyclist's shape—i.e., make it more aerodynamic—while maintaining the cyclist's riding efficiency. And just look at what taking advantage of those opportunities produces. Let's compare our typical cyclist's velocity-power profile to that of two shapes that are naturally more aerodynamic: a cylinder with a rounded leading edge and an airfoil.

HOW DOES SHAPE CHANGE THE POWER IT TAKES TO OVERCOME AIR RESISTANCE?

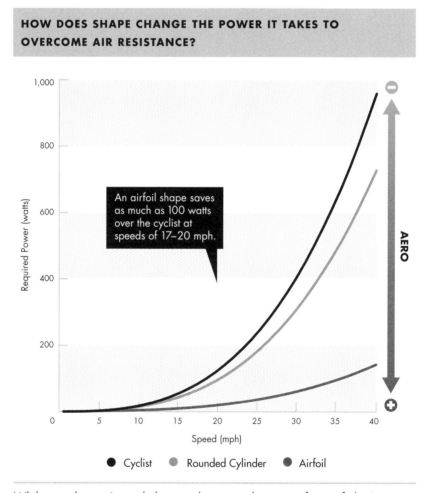

While a cyclist can't match the aerodynamic advantage of an airfoil, it's easy to see that changing the shape of an object significantly influences its aerodynamic performance.

Aerodynamics suddenly becomes much more interesting, right? If it were possible to mimic an airfoil shape, you could save as much as 100 watts at your typical speed. That's enough to bump you from 21 mph to 40 mph. Viewed another way, aerodynamics can also save significant amount of burn in your legs by the time you hit the run.

Now, 40 mph may seem like an unrealistic number, and squeezing a triathlete into the shape of an airfoil is equally unlikely. But consider the specialized enclosed recumbent bikes used in land speed record trials: They have achieved velocities in excess of 82 mph.[9] That is an incredible turn of speed. Aerodynamics isn't just a difference you can see on a graph. You can feel it.

To put this into a more practical perspective, let's compare the required power for cyclists in different cycling positions. Using a combination of wind tunnel and computer analysis methods, scientists have studied the aerodynamics of various positions and obtained a fairly reliable range of drag coefficients for each one. The graph on page 83 shows the difference between three different cycling positions. Observe how the power requirement changes as the athlete's riding position takes on a lower profile. The forward lean that occurs as the cyclist's position moves from the hoods to the drops on a road bike reduces his frontal area, making him a smaller target for air molecules. Moving the hands to the aerobars, pulling the arms in, and curving the back—in other words, achieving an optimal aerodynamic position—reduces drag even further.

Getting into a more aerodynamic shape seems simple enough. After you get into the aerobars, it stands to reason that you should buy as much gear with an airfoil profile as possible and off you go. But what seem like obvious methods aren't necessarily always the most effective. In addition, there are hundreds of aerodynamic products and as many variations in their design as there are companies making them. How do you prioritize upgrades, and how do you know you're purchasing the most effective specimen? Should you get a helmet or a more aerodynamic hydration setup? Upgrade to a better bike frame or get a disc wheel for your existing ride? Are aerodynamic tires, brake levers, and crank arms really *that* beneficial?

HOW DOES POSITION CHANGE THE POWER IT TAKES TO OVERCOME AIR RESISTANCE?

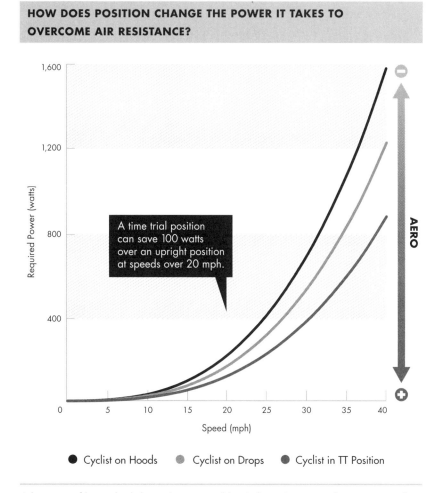

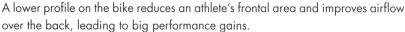

A lower profile on the bike reduces an athlete's frontal area and improves airflow over the back, leading to big performance gains.

Studies have identified the modifications that make the greatest aerodynamic contribution to performance. Although product manufacturers may disagree about nuances, their fundamental data generally agree, since wind tunnel research is widespread across academic and commercial institutions. In fact, the drag coefficients of most shapes in the field of aerodynamic study are derived experimentally. That means for any wing, wheel, or bike frame, the most accurate determination of drag coefficient (C_d) is gained in the wind tunnel. That so many shapes have had their drag coefficients measured countless times allows us to have confidence in published data. We know balls are more aerodynamic than bricks, and wings are better than both. The advent of affordable computational fluid dynamics, or CFD, gives us the added advantage of changing designs in a simulated wind tunnel without having to actually fabricate and test multiple parts. CFD saves a great deal of time and money in product development. Although a computer may not be able to match actual wind tunnel results exactly, it's close enough to prevent manufacturers from making costly mistakes in their initial design work. Given the decades of aerodynamic and bike-specific research, the numbers have become increasingly reliable.

As athletes, we can still run up against mistakes and misconceptions when we don't take a conscientious approach to changes in our aerodynamic position or equipment. Look around at your next race. You are bound to see several athletes contorting themselves into extremely unbalanced and uncomfortable positions in an effort to get lower and longer on the bike. Their new, faster position often speeds up their next visit to the chiropractor. Remember that the engine is always more important than the body. Too much emphasis on an aerodynamic position can easily cause a multitude of problems: overextension of the knees, hip angles that are inefficient for generating muscle force, reduced oxygen uptake, excessive use of upper body and core energy to maintain balance, discomfort, pulled muscles, and even nerve damage.

The least expensive triathlon-specific bikes cost more than $2,000 and some of the most advanced bike-fitting sessions are less than $500, so there's no reason why any triathlete shouldn't set aside 10 percent of her total bike budget for a proper fitting session. The potential benefits extend well beyond aerodynamics.

Strolling around the transition area you're likely to see a surprising number of bikes with high-profile wheels. This is one of the most common upgrades among athletes who want their ride to have the look of a legit tri-bike. Wheels aren't a bad idea, but when the price difference between a set of wheels or a helmet or suit can be over a thousand dollars, there are more than aerodynamic savings to think about. Before you go shopping for gear, let's get a handle on just what kind of drag savings are available.

NUMBERS IN THE REAL WORLD: BECAUSE NOBODY RACES IN A WIND TUNNEL

Up to this point, we've discussed things in terms of force and power. In Chapter 3, we related the power savings of mass by understanding that mass makes weight, and weight is a force. The language of drag savings ought to be more straightforward. It's intuitive that air exerts a force on us as we move through it. We can *feel* its force every time the wind blows. So if we can just get a measurement of that force, we can crank right through the calculations we've already performed. This will be a snap. At least, that's what we think until we start to look at actual product documentation outlining drag measurements. How often do you see the phrase "grams of drag"?

Grams?!? That's a force represented as a mass! It's about as backward as you can get, right?

For accuracy's sake, the actual unit of measurement is **kilogram-force**, which is represented as kgf. It is defined as the amount of force gravity exerts on 1 kilogram. So, according to the equation we're now familiar with:

$$F = ma$$

$$F = 1 \text{ kg} \times 9.81 \text{ m/s}^2$$

$$F = 9.81 \text{ N}$$

Seeing how the numbers work out when we multiply by 1 makes this calculation look like a waste of time. There are a couple of explanations for why we do this when measuring the aerodynamics of bicycle equipment, although none of them are particularly good. One of them deals with the history of aerodynamics, which is strongly linked to the space program. Because space exploration necessarily involves going places with different gravitational forces, scientists at NASA decided to standardize all their measurements according to Earth's gravity, also known as "g-force." Earth's gravity is 1 g. The force of gravity on the moon, Mars, in orbit, etc. is defined as some fraction of g. Aerodynamicists working in the space program always made their calculations according to g's. Later, when those engineers branched out into other industries to build recreational airplanes, race cars, and even bicycles, they simply continued using the same conventions as a matter of habit.

Even though instrumentation can measure drag forces in newtons easily enough and the conversion is simple, we still cling to the gram-force measurement, and there's a little trick at work. Notice that we're using *gram*-force and not *kilogram*-force. It takes 1,000 grams to make 1 kilogram, so when we use grams we make a small force look a lot bigger. Convert a gram-force into its equivalent in newtons to see the significance.

1 gram-force = 0.0098 newtons

If you're a product manufacturer trying to explain to people the performance improvements your design gives them, you have a choice. Which sounds better, telling people you've cut 20 grams of drag or 0.196 newtons? Grams, of course. So there's a minor mathematical sleight of hand at work in the marketing.

By converting to newtons, it suddenly looks like the drag savings on aerodynamic products are a lot smaller than what we've been led to believe . . . but don't jump to conclusions just yet. Remember that it only took a few degrees of incline to turn gravity into an overwhelming force. The first step to becoming a savvy triathlete is learning how small these forces are. The second step is being aware of just how big a difference a small force can make. Let's get a handle on the topic through some practical application. Take a look at the chart below comparing drag forces on various items of cycling equipment, and then we'll compare how their relative savings influence power.

DRAG FORCES AT WORK ON THE BIKE

ALL NUMBERS PRESENTED FOR 30 MPH (13.4 M/S) WIND TUNNEL CONDITIONS

Athlete

ATHLETE POSITION	DRAG	SAVINGS
In Road Position[10]	45 N	---
In Time Trial Position[11]	38 N	15%

Bike

BIKE MODEL	DRAG	SAVINGS
Non-Aerodynamic Road Bike[12]	9.38 N	---
Triathlon-Specific "Superbike"[13]	5.39 N	42%

Helmet

HELMET TYPE	DRAG	SAVINGS
Standard Road Helmet[14]	1.43 N	---
Time Trial Aerodynamic Helmet (best case)[15]	–0.29 N	110%
Time Trial Aerodynamic Helmet (worst case)[16]	0.32 N	77%

Wheels

WHEEL TYPE	DRAG	SAVINGS
Zipp 404, 58mm Depth[17]	1.04 N	---
Zipp 808, 81mm Depth[18]	1.00 N	3.8%
Zipp Sub-9 Disc[19]	0.85 N	18%

It's necessary to briefly remark on the *negative* drag exhibited by some time trial helmets. It's not a mistake. Indeed, the report from which these data were collected has been referenced by other researchers who have replicated the same results in independent academic research.[20] Negative drag has also been witnessed during tests on some disc wheels.[21] Although it's not typical, it does happen, most frequently with helmets. The explanation for this is not that the helmet itself possesses some magical property that allows it to defy physics. By itself, an aero helmet would actually have significant drag because it would scoop air like an upside-down bowl. But when you use it as prescribed (that is, put it on your head), things change. The bowl of the helmet gets filled in, and your head takes on a different shape. Wind tunnel tests have demonstrated that the human head is not aerodynamic, and that a time trial helmet reduces drag significantly. Because these tests put the helmet on the head of a mannequin and then subtract the drag contribution of the dummy's head, we wind up with a negative value. That means the helmet is producing an aerodynamic force that actually *pushes* you (the opposite of drag is propulsion)! But don't curse helmet manufacturers for lying to you if you don't feel like your helmet is pushing you forward during your next race. Thanks to your head, the total drag of the head-helmet combo remains positive.

With the issue of negative drag taken care of, let's take a look at the bigger picture with regard to drag savings. The savings percentages are included in the chart for a reason. We often see product manufacturers describe fantastic performance improvements over competitors. Fifty percent sounds like a huge leap, and in some respects, it is. When you get a piece of equipment as refined as modern top-end triathlon gear, it takes substantial time, brainpower, and money to find even an extra 5 percent improvement. This is the driving force behind the emergence of collaborative efforts between bicycle companies and some of the biggest names in automotive racing. Professional athletes routinely visit wind tunnels used by NASCAR to refine their positioning. The bike maker Specialized and exotic car manufacturer McLaren worked together to develop the aerodynamic Venge bike, and Honda teamed with Parlee to develop a unique aerodynamic concept bike. But aside from the extraordinary investment, what's the real benefit? What does that 50 percent improvement translate to on the race clock?

The answer lies in the raw number expressing the actual drag force. We save 7 newtons by transferring from a typical road race position to a time trial position. An aero helmet supposedly saves 1 newton. But we still have to qualify things, even when we talk in terms of these raw numbers. Note that all drag values here were measured for headwinds of 30 mph. That's an optimistically high speed for many triathletes to hold for a long period of time. We can imagine a scenario where you're riding at a speed of 20 mph into a 10 mph headwind. In such a case, the total effect of the wind would equate to 30 mph (for a closer look at how yaw angles work, see the Brace Yourselves section, pages 93–98). Even this is a stretch, seeing as how estimates of the average wind speed in any direction in North America range between 6 and 9 mph. It's safe to say that racing at 30 mph is only probable for a select group of elite triathletes, so why the 30 mph convention?

Manufacturers and researchers perform their tests at 30 mph because of the way sensors in wind tunnels work. For engineers to ensure that forces can be measured with a reasonable degree of certainty, it's best to use the highest wind speed possible. The lower the wind speed, the smaller the forces become and the more sensitive the equipment has to be. The percentages will remain the same, so getting the measurement right at a high speed is what matters most to the engineers when they are trying to improve a design.

Nevertheless, *in the world of triathlon a relative wind speed of 20–25 mph is the more likely scenario*. The force of the wind against an object will be much lower at that speed (see the graph on page 80), and although the percentages will still be the same, the actual drag savings will be much less.

With that in the back of our minds, let's do a quick math check before we get too carried away about the relative advantages of one product over another. How about we take our various components listed in the chart and put them to a theoretical test by adding up their drag values? That will provide us with the total resistive aerodynamic force against a rider at 30 mph. Using that specific force at that speed, we can then get an estimate for the power required for each setup.

To do that, we'll take a look at three different athletes. Our first is an average triathlete riding a standard road bike in a typical road position with a common set of aero wheels and a road helmet. Our second triathlete has all the top-end aerodynamic gear (superbike, disc wheel, aero helmet) and remains in the time trial position. Our third triathlete has all the same upgrades as the second triathlete, but because he didn't get a good fit he will sit up in a road position. Just to be clear, we're talking about the power required only to *overcome* aerodynamic forces. First, we add up the resistive forces on each rider:

TRIATHLETE	SETUP	POWER TO OVERCOME RESTRICTIVE FORCE*
Average	road bike, road position	57.85 N
Top-Dollar Aero	superbike, time trial position	44.95 N
Poorly fitted	superbike, road position	51.95 N
*ALL NUMBERS PRESENTED FOR 30 MPH (13.4 M/S) WIND TUNNEL CONDITIONS		

With some quick computing, our work and power equations help us figure out the required power for each triathlete:

$$P = Fv$$

TRIATHLETE	SETUP	POWER TO OVERCOME AERO FORCES*
Average	road bike, road position	775.8 W
Top-Dollar Aero	superbike, time trial position	602.8 W
Poorly Fitted	superbike, road position	696.7 W
*ALL NUMBERS PRESENTED FOR 30 MPH (13.4 M/S) WIND TUNNEL CONDITIONS		

And our results are . . . *completely unrealistic.* It is not uncommon for professional cyclists to ride at speeds over 30 mph during time trials, yet they never produce this much power. So what gives?

The force of drag is never as high as the numbers we established on page 90. We took the *sum* of the forces of different components, but those forces were established for each component on an individual basis. Figuring out the forces on a fully assembled bike is much more complicated than finding the sum of the parts. When all of the parts come together, drafting factors in. Much like a group of cyclists riding in a peloton, the individual bike components are "drafting" each other. The bike drafts the front wheel and the rear wheel drafts the bike. Aerodynamic interactions between those parts at the front of the bike drastically influence drag on parts farther to the rear. Engineers refer to the steady, undisturbed state of the air prior to hitting the bike as "clean" air. After its initial impact with a surface (tire, bike frame, or rider), the airflow becomes "dirty," or chaotic in terms of its velocity and direction. **The total apparatus of bike and rider actually winds up with about half of the drag we calculate.** When it comes to bike aerodynamics, the whole is *not* greater than the sum of its parts. It's a different animal altogether.

This leads us to wonder if there's any accuracy (or truth) in advertising. It's apparent that some components wind up experiencing less drag than their advertised value, and it is therefore possible that other components experience more drag, depending on how a bike is set up. Furthermore, the shape of a complete bike is so complex that it becomes prohibitively time consuming and expensive even for CFD to create accurate simulations. The only way to get a precise measurement of how equipment changes affect the overall performance of a bike is to swap them out in successive wind tunnel tests. This brings us back to the expensive and time-consuming process that CFD was originally designed to avoid: multiple iterative tests in a wind tunnel.

There are two significant lessons to be learned from this exercise. First, while the 30 mph scenario is a great test level for the wind tunnel, it does not accurately reflect real-world conditions for most triathletes. Normann Stadler's Ironman Hawaii bike course record of 4:18:23 "only" gave him a 26 mph average speed. Winds during the day remained constant from the north, balancing out their influence on his performance on the generally north-south course, but it is reasonable to assume that quite often he experienced relative headwinds in excess of 30 mph.[22] Time trial stages in professional cycling races exhibit these speeds much more frequently but are generally no longer than 40 km, which is much shorter than long-distance triathlons. Once a triathlete accounts for the relative power-saving benefit of a product in a context more appropriate to her sport and the particular course she's competing on, she can decide whether the benefit is worth the financial expense. Once again, use the rule of thumb that 10 watts will save you approximately 40–60 seconds over a distance of 25 miles.

The second major lesson is not to assume that every equipment item will improve your aerodynamics on the bike by the advertised amount. It's fair to say that the equipment will have *some* benefit. No one designs a product with the intent of making you slower. But it is simply not cost effective for manufacturers to test their products with multiple combinations of other components. Therefore, it remains somewhat of a mystery *how much* of an advantage different components afford us.

HEADS UP: THE FINER POINTS ABOUT AERO HELMETS

We've already seen a general comparison demonstrating the advantages provided by aerodynamically shaped time trial helmets. However, there are significant variations within this form of design. Air vents, visors, and unique tail lengths not only give helmets distinctive appearances but offer differing performance characteristics as well. Thankfully, research shows that there are some fundamental aspects of aerodynamics that indicate superior design.

First, and perhaps most surprising, is that air vents in the front of a helmet make a negligible contribution to its drag. That means that triathletes don't have to sacrifice ventilation for speed.[23]

The second important finding from research is that helmets with shorter tails and steeper taper angles perform better than helmets with long tails that come to a sharper tip.[24]

Finally, though apparently of least interest to triathletes based on their choice of helmets, is that data conflicts on whether visors make a positive contribution to a helmet's performance. The qualification here is that a visor only seems to work to your advantage so long as you are in the time trial position. More research is needed to understand this observation, but for the time being it appears fashion is driving athletes' decisions about making the switch to these helmets.[25] On the whole, this leaves athletes with a good basic approach to making their choice: Seek out a helmet that has a shorter, blunter endpoint and don't worry about sacrificing ventilation. Dimples, visors, and other gimmicks may not make you faster, but they won't make you particularly slower, either. So long as you get the basic shape right, you'll be making a smart selection.

BRACE YOURSELVES, WINDS ARE COMING: CROSSWINDS AND THEIR EFFECTS ON CYCLING

Up to this point our discussion of aerodynamics has dealt with the less-than-ideal condition of pedaling into the wind. However, we're all aware that isn't the only condition we encounter on a bike. More often than not, it feels like wind comes at us from every direction. So how do we account for that?

Let's begin with what we know intuitively. Time trial gear is made to cut through the wind in the direction we're going, like a hot knife cuts through butter. We try to make our profile long and narrow like an airplane wing. But look at a bike from the side, and our "knifelike" appearance suddenly resembles the sail on a boat. It acts that way when the wind hits us from the

When the wind is blowing directly against your direction of travel, the total perceived wind velocity is the wind speed added to the bike speed.

side, too. The same goes for our wheels. The front wheel can make things especially tricky if the rim is deep. At a sufficiently high velocity, wind can hit a wheel as hard as a baseball bat and send you off into a ditch. These are just a few of the reasons manufacturers have become more concerned in recent years with designing products to contend with crosswinds. In the past, wind conditions on the racecourse had a significant impact on a triathlete's equipment choices. At the notoriously windy Ironman World Championships, some professional contenders would even give up their aero helmets for traditional road cycling headgear, and high-profile aero wheels with more than 61 mm of rim depth were unheard of. Although aero helmets and deep rims cut through the air as triathletes pedal into the wind, they threaten to carry competitors off the road and into the lava fields when crosswinds strike. Dealing with crosswinds indirectly by altering your gear makes you faster because it helps you maintain control of the bike at speed.

Observe the figure above. Typically, we think of air resistance occurring when air hits us directly from the front. The total velocity of the headwind is the sum of our velocity and the wind's velocity. This is the simplest concept of air resistance, though, and both the wind and cyclists are wont to frequently change directions.

The other simplified concept of wind condition is a "perfect" cross-wind, or one that blows directly from the side. We show this in the figure below. Things get a little more complicated here. Even when the wind itself exerts no force directly against us, we still feel a headwind equal to our speed. That headwind and crosswind combine to form a new force that we call the **effective crosswind**. The important thing to understand about effective crosswind is that it not only creates resistance, it also causes complicated control and stability issues. Anyone who's ridden the bike leg at Ironman Couer d'Alene or the Queen K knows how substantial this can be. Things become more complicated once you get into crosswind angles between 0 and 90 degrees. Several factors must be accounted for, including wind speed and angle, and the cyclist's velocity. These elements influence a new factor for consideration: the angle between the cyclist and the effective crosswind, properly known as the **yaw angle**.

RESISTANCE IN CROSSWINDS

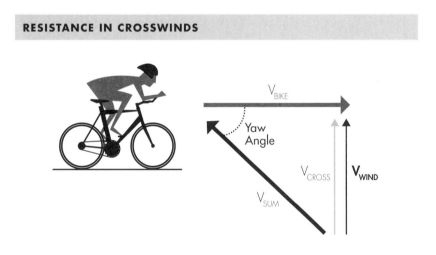

When wind comes in directly from the side, the crosswind is equal to the wind speed. The headwind speed is equal to the bike speed. But the apparent wind is greater than the two components, and it feels like it comes in from an angle.

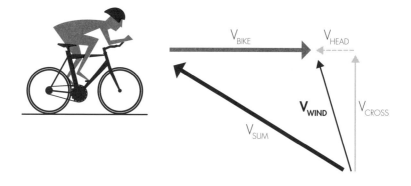

Wind coming in from different angles changes both the perceived wind velocity and direction.

Manufacturers design products to various standards. Depending on their perception of how important crosswind performance is (and just how forceful crosswinds can be), they may test products at yaw angles of 10, 20, or even 35 degrees. The rationale among some is that you rarely pedal into a direct headwind, so being more aerodynamic in a crosswind makes sense. But even good science can be taken too far, and some design approaches to crosswinds do exactly that. One might think that it only makes sense to be effective at the highest yaw angle possible. If you're good to go at 30 degrees, you'll be even better at 10, right? Actually, no. The problem is that even though *winds* may hit a cyclist from any angle, the cyclist herself always moves forward. So the emphasis on cutting air resistance must necessarily be optimized for that direction. It's impossible to make a shape aerodynamic at all possible angles. The key to success for designers is to make the product for the most likely range of winds the triathlete or cyclist will encounter, and the key for you is to know which designers are doing that. For a product manufacturer, that means figuring out the wind speed and angle the athlete will see most frequently on the racecourse. Collecting data to figure out the average speed and direction of winds in North America would take years of research and hundreds of thousands of dollars. Thankfully, the National Weather Service has been keeping this data for decades. Reports yield the following probability of encountering crosswinds of the corresponding angles at 30 mph.[26]

YAW ANGLE	PROBABILITY
0°	100%
2.5°	61%
5°	29%
7.5°	15%
10°	8%
15°	1%
20°	0%

In light of this, a product designed to account for crosswinds of 20 degrees may not be best suited for real-world conditions. ***The most likely range of crosswind yaw angles is less than 10 degrees.***

Narrowing the band of crosswind yaw angles for which a product is developed allows designers greater freedom to optimize performance in the straightforward direction, which is exactly what the athlete wants. When looking at different equipment items, take the time to look at the data from the manufacturers. Many of them routinely publish their wind tunnel research, including drag at specific yaw angles. By observing what range of angles they focused on and how the product performed, you can learn a great deal about the quality of their method and design.

The biggest factor in determining these proportions is the speed of the bike itself. As can be seen in the figure on page 98, the faster you go the more the apparent wind angle decreases, so in a way you turn a crosswind into more of a headwind. This doesn't decrease the magnitude of the side force the crosswind exerts on you, but it does increase the force working against your forward motion.

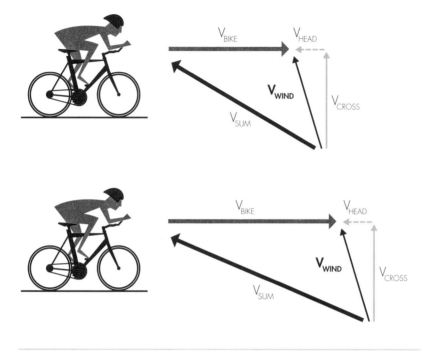

As rider speed increases, the apparent wind velocity (V_{sum}) increases and the apparent yaw angle decreases.

At the end of the day, there is only so much you can do about crosswinds. Just as with headwinds, they have more of an influence on the rider than the bike. You can't redesign yourself to deal with crosswinds better, but avoiding equipment choices that complicate matters will help you keep the bike rubber-side down, and that's always a surefire means of improving your time. Be aware of how products account for crosswinds in their design parameters, but don't let yourself get carried away by over-zealous advertising.

LORD OF THE RIMS: A DISCUSSION OF WHEELS THAT COMES FULL CIRCLE

Wheels are a perplexing phenomenon in triathlon. It seems that no triathlon bike is truly complete without a set of high-profile aerodynamic wheels. In the modern world of speed weapons, they are the heavy artillery. And, let's face it, they make your bike look extra cool. Aero wheels can also cost half as much as your entire bike, making the purchase a big decision. What makes them such a necessary item, and is one design better than another?

The benefit of aerodynamic wheels is best demonstrated by their most extreme incarnation. Disc wheels, which appear as one solid piece instead of a rim supported by spokes extending from the hub, cut down on drag by filling in a significant empty space along the rear wheel. This prevents the development of vortices; instead, the air is guided along the surface of the wheel in a smoother flow. The concept behind disc wheels is very similar to that of the fully enclosed bikes that are used to attempt land speed records. The more you can create a solid, smooth surface for the air to travel along, the fewer holes and gaps there are to create drag. This is why indoor track cyclists often use discs for both their front and rear wheels. They can get away with it because there are no crosswinds indoors. Outside, they'd be blown off the track by only a slight gust.

Triathletes ride in a wide variety of outdoor conditions. Sometimes you can use a rear disc wheel, but most of the time wind conditions preclude it. This is what first led manufacturers to develop an array of wheels with varying rim depths. Rim depth is measured as the distance from the outermost area of the rim to the innermost. Measurements are made in millimeters. Common depths range from 46 mm to 100 mm. Seeing the advantages of a full disc wheel has led to the conventional wisdom that a deeper wheel is a faster one. But like a disc wheel, a high-profile wheel is more troublesome in windy conditions.

Those are the fundamental principles. Upon those foundations engineers and scientists have sought to make aerodynamic improvements for the benefit of triathletes and time trialists. They have modified the shape and width of wheels and even experimented with the profile and number of spokes supporting the rim. What follows is a brief overview of those innovations, a quick examination of what research has yet to be conducted in wheel technology, and what it means to the weekend-warrior triathlete.

Deeper

Intuition tells you that deeper rims will reduce drag as the wheel shape approaches that of a disc wheel. It's just a little more complicated than that. Wind tunnel data indicate that in a direct headwind, wheels with less rim depth actually have a slight advantage. Once crosswinds reach a slight yaw angle, however, the deeper wheels perform much better. Of course, that comes with the aforementioned penalty of the destabilizing forces imposed on us by crosswinds. Our "speed weapon" is a double-edged sword.[27]

Wider

The idea behind making wide rims even wider actually stems from the tire. Wheel designers used to simply try to make the fastest wheel without considering how the tire itself would influence airflow. Once it occurred to them that the tire was an unavoidable issue, they found something interesting. The conventional wisdom in aerodynamics is that thinner is faster. This is why supersonic jets like the SR-71 and the Concorde were so needle-nosed. But in the case of wheels, the tire acts as the nose. The narrower the wheel, the more comparatively bulbous the nose (tire) becomes. "Skinny" is a relative term. It's better to be wider and have a more streamlined shape than be thin with a lumpy protrusion. By making the rim wider, the tire fits onto the rim with less bulge, thus making it easier for air to flow over it.

Blunter

Taking a page from bike-frame and helmet designers' playbooks, some wheel manufacturers have chopped off their wheels' "tails" in favor of a more rounded endpoint to their rims. This move occurred for several reasons. One was to offset forces created by crosswinds on deeper-profile wheels. Another was to help reduce instability at high speeds. More-rounded rims are one of the most significant recent developments in wheels because the forces on the front wheel influence the overall stability and handling of the bike.

What does it all add up to? Honestly, not much. There is no end to the independent tests and academic papers that have cropped up around this very question, but instead of seeking obscure journal articles it would be much easier for you to simply go to the manufacturers yourself. Visit the web site of just about any major manufacturer of wheels used on triathlon bikes and you're likely to find a page dedicated to their technology and aerodynamics research. Browse through their tables and graphs and pick the drag values for a few different wheels at one or two yaw angles (remember which ones count!). Use the conversion factors you've learned to change grams of drag into force (1 gram-force = 0.0098 newton), and then multiply that force by velocity (13.4 m/s, the metric equivalent of 30 mph) to find the actual power required to drive a wheel at that velocity. Then it's a simple matter of subtraction to figure out how much different wheels save you.

What you'll find is that there is virtually no difference between competing brands at equivalent rim depths, and that rim depth only makes a significant difference in a very narrow range of yaw angles. On top of that, you have to keep in mind that these are measurements taken on a wheel that is *not* attached to a bicycle. In terms of drag reduction, this is the best-case scenario.

Remember, too, that the rear wheel of your bike operates in totally different conditions from the front wheel. It continues to draft behind the bike and your churning legs, making aero gains hard to quantify, let alone improve in a definitive way. A disc might make a useful difference; a deep rim, not so much.

In sum, a set of aero wheels can save you as much as 20 watts over the standard pair that came with your bike. That's the best-case scenario. *When you start comparing different brands or levels of aero wheels, the advantage may not even achieve the 10-watt threshold established as our rule of thumb.*

This rolls back into our original theory of relativity: Every improvement and advantage on the bike is relative. In our cyborg fusion of man and machine from Chapter 3, the man provides the majority of the body's weight and aerodynamics. The bike is only a fraction of the body, and the wheels are only a fraction of the bike. In terms of mass and aerodynamics, they don't merit a high placement on the list of equipment priorities.

LAW & ORDER, CFD: INVESTIGATING THE CASE OF THE DUELING WIND TUNNEL TESTS

Dueling wind tunnel tests are a subject of perennial aggravation for triathletes looking for the fastest cycling gear on the market. Over the years, manufacturers have released several reports, called white papers, showing the results of head-to-head wind tunnel tests between their products and those of their competitors. Discriminating consumers who take the time to compare these reports quickly realize what you might expect: Company A and company B sharply disagree on whose model is best. Things get even trickier when you observe what A and B say about company C. The numbers are so far apart that it's hard to tell which report is the most accurate, if any of them are accurate at all. To be sure, there will always be a level of bias involved when a product manufacturer performs a test. But the disparity in the results can generally be explained, and these explanations matter to athletes who want to understand their equipment.

Once we start talking about comparative aerodynamic tests and competitive brands, everything we discussed previously about the reliability of the wind tunnel starts to feel a little hollow. If the information and methods are so tried and true, how do competing companies turn them into contradictory data sets?

Fear not. No one is paying off the guys running the wind tunnels. The data still offer good information and the numbers don't lie. But charts and graphs can obstruct your investigation of who made the better product. The key is to realize that graphs aren't exactly numbers. They're more like artistic interpretations of data. Depending on how much artistic license is taken, you can end up with a rather creative interpretation of the facts. In the case of the dueling wind tunnel tests, you may need to put the numbers under bright lights and look at them with a magnifying glass. Now that you know the math and science behind cycling product development, don't allow yourself to simply accept two lines on a graph showing a big difference between brands. Consider for a moment how we've used graphs throughout this chapter. In each case, we have used the graph to express a trend, and then picked out specific numbers to assess the significance of that trend or value. Be careful of the chart or graph followed by the declaration "The results speak for themselves." Allowing results to speak for themselves is a little like refusing counsel and defending yourself in court. It's ill-advised and often leads to trouble. Similarly, why would a manufacturer simply rest its case after showing you Exhibit A? Wouldn't a brand interested in making a really strong case for you to buy its product continue to lay on the proof and explain exactly what it is you are looking at? Why not take the time to put into context its product's drag savings so you can truly appreciate the value? Not providing thorough information is a good clue that the company's case isn't that strong to begin with. Turn on the bright lights and get out the magnifying glass.

Scrutinize how the graph is laid out, especially when hard numbers aren't available. An ant can look like a monster if you look at it under a microscope.

Look carefully at the scale of units. Is the scale on the bottom and side of the graph magnifying small differences? Is it making a very small difference appear large? You'll probably have to calculate power from grams of drag to figure that out. That leads to your second clue.

Consider the clarity and precision of the data. How easy is it to determine an accurate drag value at a particular yaw angle or speed from a manufacturer's graph? Do you have to estimate whether a number is between 350 and 360, or between 350 and 400? If the former is the case, ask yourself why would anyone make a graph so difficult to read?

The answers to these questions begin to pull back the curtain on bike industry marketing. But this premise remains: Product manufacturers do not set out to design a worse product and then fool you into buying it. They go to market believing in the product they are selling. Is their brand better? In their eyes, absolutely. What's at stake is just how much better the product is. The answer is often "Not better enough to count."

The answers to these questions begin to pull back the curtain on bike industry marketing. But this premise remains: Product manufacturers do not set out to design a worse product and then fool you into buying it. They go to market believing in the product they are selling. Is their brand better? In their eyes, absolutely. The question is just how much better the product is. The answer is often "Not better enough to count." It's usually the case that the improvement in question doesn't push the product, or its overall contribution to your performance, over the 10-watt threshold that's our rule of thumb. And this is why the winner in the case of the dueling wind tunnels often remains an unsolved mystery.

Let's say you conduct a wind tunnel test on a set of items to figure out their aerodynamic differences. Take a cube, a sphere, and a bike helmet. Your results will be pretty reliable. In other words, if someone ran the same experiment in a different wind tunnel on the other side of the world, their numbers would be pretty close to yours and you'd both agree on which object was most aerodynamic. Now let's say you assessed three helmets of varying design. Things get more complicated. Depending on the size and shape of the mannequin head you put the helmets on, how the helmet is placed on the head, and how tightly you adjust the straps, you could come up with a different winner than your counterpart does. Differences in instrumentation and test protocols can make for significant experimental errors, and if the helmet designs are very similar to each other, then your margin of error isn't large at all. The issue of complexity is most difficult when testing complete bikes. **When the leading superbikes at the cutting-edge of technology square off in the wind tunnel, the difference between them will be a tiny fraction of their total drag.** A wind tunnel is an extraordinarily accurate device, but it still has its limitations.

This is how it is possible for product manufacturers to disagree with each other and still be honest with you. If they all agreed on how items should be tested, what aspects of aerodynamic design should be optimized, and what makes the best product, then they'd all make the *same* bike, helmet, or wheel. Their products win in their tests because that's the test they built their product to win. Meanwhile, some other manufacturer is looking at the competition and trying to figure out how to beat them in *their own* test. Manufacturers are essentially telling you that "Brand X is the undisputed champion of the Brand X championships."

It may feel good to know they're generally honest (as long as they're making a strong enough argument for themselves), but that doesn't help you close the case. You're still left with a lineup of products and no clear indication of which one you should pick. This is when you, as investigator, have to interrogate the reports in separate rooms and determine which reports corroborate each other and which numbers don't add up. The key is *consistency*. Oftentimes competing brands will test each other's products in comparative tests. When your choices are narrowed to a few major brands, see if they've run tests against each other (or if third-party brands have run tests on them), and then compare the graphs for consistency. *Whichever product performs the best over the widest range of tests is most likely your winner.*

WHERE THE RUBBER HITS THE ROAD: CAN MY CHOICE OF TIRES REALLY MAKE ME FASTER?

We end our scientific exploration of the triathlete's bicycle the same way most triathletes end their trip to the bike shop, with a quick discussion of tires. After everything else we do at the bike shop, we remember, "Oh, yeah! I need some tires." It's funny that such an important component of our ride comes as an afterthought. Even more peculiar is how shops often arrange them, tucked away in some obscure corner between the tools and degreaser without fanfare in their little nondescript boxes. This is terribly unfortunate, because after everything else we've discussed, your choice of tires is one of the few places where you can get a legitimate speed bonus without spending a great deal of money or time. Tires and tubes may remain last on your checklist, but don't breeze by and grab something off the shelf. Do a little homework beforehand and you'll make the most of your purchase.

This homework is not difficult. We are looking at one discriminating factor when it comes to tire design: rolling resistance. It is the most frequently tested quality in tire manufacturing and considered the benchmark of quality. That is not to say it is the only factor, but the others are either insignificant or predetermined by your wheel choice. Once we are familiar with the landscape we can see how rolling resistance converts to power and speed.

Tires come in three varieties: clincher, tubular, and open tubular.

Clincher tires are the most ubiquitous in cycling. The tire and tube are separate from each other and are held fast against the wheel by the shape of the rim, tension in the tire, and the pressure from the inflated tube.

Tubular tires have an integrated tube held inside the tire with stitching. They require glue to hold them to the wheel.

Open tubular tires are essentially hybrid tubulars that have not been stitched up to hold the tube inside, so they behave like a clincher. This may sound confusing until you understand that the type of tire you use is specific to your wheel.

Tubular tires only work on tubular wheels. Clincher tires only work on clincher wheels. Open tubular tires only work on clincher wheels. This begs some questions: Why two different types of tires for the same type of wheel? Why does the hybrid mix the two types if it doesn't fit on both types of wheels? Open tubulars were designed to exhibit the best performance characteristics of both worlds. Comparatively speaking, conventional cycling wisdom says that tubular tires are lighter, more efficient, and more puncture-resistant than clincher tires. On the other hand, clincher tires are cheaper, easier to fix, and do not require the messy glue work to attach them to the wheel. For decades, professional cyclists and triathletes have used tubular tires for a speed advantage, whereas clincher tires have remained the go-to option of weekend warriors. Open tubulars are constructed to be as light and fast as tubulars without the time and mess. Think of them as top-notch clinchers.

There's been an awful lot written in books and magazines about the relative differences in tire type and developments in tire technology. Manufacturers constantly try to improve resilience, weight, and aerodynamics through varying chemical and textile processes to manipulate the tire's inherent properties and interaction with the wheel. By and large, the point is moot. For starters, the overwhelming majority of triathletes use clincher wheels, which means tubular tires don't even enter into the discussion. For those who do use tubulars, the relative advantages in weight are miniscule. Come race day, you would have to make sure your sports bar weighs less than whatever your competition puts in her back pocket to secure the advantage. The same goes for aerodynamic considerations. We've already discussed that **wheels amount to a fraction of a fraction of the total aerodynamic drag of our cyclist. Tires are a fraction of a fraction of a fraction**. In other words, the benefit is a rounding error. In the final analysis, most triathletes choose clincher wheels and use either clincher or open tubular tires because they simply don't want to deal with the hassle of regular tubulars. Regardless of your choice, you've already narrowed your range of tire options, which is actually rather advantageous. Depending on how you roll, there is a distinction in quality and speed. It's time to talk about rolling resistance.

Rolling resistance occurs as a result of a tire's interaction with the ground. Just like your hands paddling through the water or your bike pushing through the air, the interaction between body and medium is not 100 percent efficient. Some energy is lost at the contact point between the two. These losses come in three forms: the deformation of your tire at the contact point with the ground, a minor amount of slipping that occurs between the ground and any object that comes into contact with it, and a form of vibration known as hysteresis.

The deformation of the tire is the easiest to understand. Sit on your bike and you'll notice that the tires squish a little bit, no matter how well-inflated they are. Contact with the ground causes the tire to conform to the road and flatten out, but otherwise your tire maintains a rounded shape. As the tire rolls forward, the portion that comes into contact with the ground begins to squish flat. This process is constantly occurring and takes energy. To observe it firsthand, squish the top of your tire with your thumb. The force you exert to do it takes energy. The tire can also lose its frictional hold on the ground at times, which bleeds energy. Think of it as spinning out on a microscopic scale. You don't notice it, and even on a scientific level it's a negligible consideration.

The final matter of hysteresis is quite observable, and does make a noticeable contribution to energy losses. Even if you traditionally like a little music to accompany you on your ride, you've hopefully taken the head-phones off at least once to take in the sounds of nature around you. If you pay attention, you'll become aware of a constant hum in the background. Your entire bike contributes to making that noise. Like a guitar channeling vibrations, the bike's hollow frame amplifies the vibrations to the point that they excite the air molecules around the bike and broadcast sound waves you can hear. Because of its properties and structure, carbon fiber makes for a more pronounced sound, but the actual source of the vibration is your tires.

Every second, the tires make dozens of impacts with tiny particles on the road, the molecular equivalent of tiny fingers plucking guitar strings. Without small particles and cracks that make its surface rough, the road would be as slick as ice and you would slip off. We need the traction that texture provides us. But the vibration it causes in your bike is a pesky drain on energy that would be better spent on moving forward. Although we can't control how rough the pavement gets, we can choose tires that are most resilient to the conditions. The measure of that resilience is the **coefficient of rolling resistance**, defined as the proportion of applied force to the amount of resisting force.[28]

$$C_{rr} = \frac{F_r}{F_a}$$

Where C_{rr} is the coefficient of rolling resistance, F_r is resistive force, and F_a is applied force.

This proportion leads to very small numbers (usually less than 0.0030 for bicycle tires), but it allows for a standardized comparison across types. A further boon to triathletes is the relatively inexpensive process of testing for rolling resistance. Thanks to frequent tests by independent publications and magazines, we have easy access to the most up-to-date information on which tires perform best.

This brings us to the ultimate question: Just how much faster can a good tire be? Let's examine how rolling resistance is related to power and calculate how many watts we save given a difference in tires. The power required to overcome rolling resistance is directly related to speed, and is given by the equation:

$$P = m \times g \times v \times C_{rr}$$

*Where **P** is power, **m** is mass, **g** is acceleration of gravity, **v** is velocity, and **C_{rr}** is the coefficient of rolling resistance.*

With that in mind, let's compare a group of tires as tested by independent researcher Alan Morrison in 2010 for his web site Bike Tech Review. Below are the best and worst tires in the test. Keep in mind that the Specialized open tubular is actually a clincher tire.[29]

TUBE/TIRE	C_{RR}
Vittoria Pista Evo CS Tubular	0.00220
Specialized Mondo Open Tubular (Michelin Latex Tube)	0.00233
Tufo S33 Special	0.00467
Conti GP 3000	0.00488

Using the equation above, we find the relationship between power and velocity for each tire, and the result is quite significant. At 20 mph, the Vittoria and Specialized tires require 14 and 15 watts of power to overcome rolling resistance. The Tufo and Conti tires require 30 and 32 watts, respectively, at the same speed. This more than meets the 10 watt standard set forth by our cycling power rule of thumb. ***The difference between the absolute best and some of the worst tires is about 40–60 seconds per every 25 miles.*** This ought to emphasize the matter for those triathletes who pick whatever tires are cheapest or simply choose colors that match their bike in their rush to get out of the shop. Take an extra few minutes

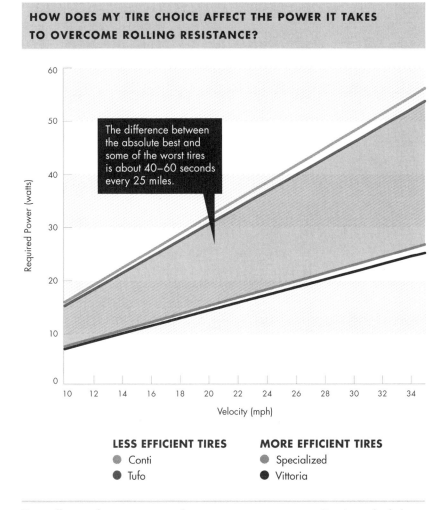

Tires affect performance as much as some aero equipment. Don't overlook them.

at home to figure out which tires are best, and you might get into T2 a few minutes sooner!

The observant triathlete probably noticed there's a mass term in the equation for rolling resistance, meaning that weight influences the force acting against their tires. Does this revive the argument to shave grams

DOES WEIGHT AFFECT THE POWER IT TAKES TO OVERCOME ROLLING RESISTANCE?

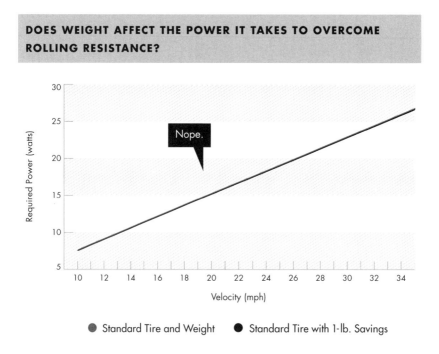

Nope.

Required Power (watts) vs. Velocity (mph)

● Standard Tire and Weight ● Standard Tire with 1-lb. Savings

Again, mass is not a great factor. You improve rolling resistance more with tire choice than with lighter equipment.

off the bike? Let's compare the resistance on the same set of tires at different applied weights. Assume you could drop a pound somewhere. You can see in the graph above that the difference is so small that the plots of required power are barely distinguishable.

Before closing, there are a few other tidbits of information you may find useful in your racing and training. Research indicating that rough roads increase rolling resistance by up to 44 percent has been cited in other works, but the studies are incomplete and have not been replicated.[30] Tire pressure is also a factor. *As tire pressure increases, the coefficient of rolling resistance decreases dramatically until a pressure of 110 psi is reached. After that you reach the point of diminishing returns and risk making your ride very bumpy.*[31]

THESE AREN'T THE UPGRADES YOU'RE LOOKING FOR: STOP WORRYING ABOUT "OTHER LOSSES"

We mentioned "other losses" in Chapter 3 and then spent our entire time discussing the "stuff that matters." But just because something is negligible isn't license for us to be negligent. It's as helpful to know what a bad decision looks like as it is to understand a good one. So what have we not discussed and why?

The primary reason we haven't looked at the following issues in depth is quite simply because they're not worth our time. In the great big world of improvements in cycling performance, triathletes have bigger gains to chase down. On an individual basis, the following items are almost always (and we leave room for even the smallest possibility) more costly than they are worth on a dollar-per-watt basis.

High-Performance Bearings

From time to time independent manufacturers mention high-performance bearings, but for the most part bike companies already use high-quality bearings in their bottom brackets and wheel hubs. High-grade bearings are used in a wide range of products beyond cycling, and as such are cost-effective to produce and incorporate in bicycle designs. Special "upgraded bearing" options on bike components are a waste of time and money.

Chain Lube

The difference between competing brands of lubricant is also negligible. Although there are differences in chain design and construction, the primary determinant of frictional losses in your bike chain is not what oil you used, but how well you cleaned the chain. A clean chain will always run better than a dirty one. It is very easy to have your bike shop show you how to install a quick-link device on your chain. This link will allow you to remove your chain from your bike without special tools. You can then give the chain a thorough cleaning and even let it soak in solvent for a bit. This will ensure all the fine grit and grease come off before you put it back on. Afterward, a thin coat of any kind of oil will suffice. Lubricants and waxes advertising performance improvements usually claim around 5–8 watts in savings in a best-case scenario, and your chain is only going to get dirty again the farther you go. Skip the high-dollar treatments on a component you replace regularly. Use the quick-link and keep it clean.

Skin Suits, Unique Fabrics, Extreme Hydration System Setups, Shaved Legs

All pretty questionable. What works for one person or bike may not work for another. Except for the shaved legs. That doesn't work for anyone. If you really want to make a last-minute attachment modification that counts, take a look inside your athlete's packet after race check-in. That big race number they give you to wear on your back and strap around your bike's seat post? Ever heard the term "drag flag"? Well, now you have. It didn't cost you a dime, and it can waive (pun intended) all those aforementioned little aero advantages. Some very innovative people noticed this aggravating phenomenon, and there are now several good solutions available on the market for triathletes interested in a bolt-on solution to hold their number in place.

That's it. If we haven't talked about it, you really don't need to worry about it. You have everything you need to propel you to the utmost of your potential and all the success you can get on the bike. By the time you're ready to get more detailed than the concepts covered here, you'll probably be meeting with the engineers at your sponsor's headquarters to discuss how to win a world championship. But no matter how bad you blister the field on the bike, you're not going to make that meeting unless you follow up your ride with a solid run. So let's make a quick transition to our third and final discipline. Giddy up!

CHAPTER 5

THE RUN

WHETHER IT'S STEPHEN HAWKING considering the nature of black holes or a bicycle engineer with a degree in physics looking at wind tunnel data, a scientist can spend his entire life trying to explain one aspect of the universe around us. Hopefully there will come a day when he exclaims, "Of course!" a blissful moment when it all comes together and the math makes perfect sense. In the world of engineering, these epiphanies are often referred to as eureka moments. Athletes know them better as breaking through a plateau. There's not a great difference; an athlete's physical pain in training to break through a performance plateau is similar to the mental frustration a scientist endures in his quest for revelation. In both cases, sometimes the breakthrough requires a new way of looking at things.

As triathletes, we try to improve our running by changing the equation to create the result we want. We go on long runs to extend our aerobic base. We go on interval runs to increase our threshold. We go on tempo runs to increase our speed. We do drills to improve our running form. But have you ever gone on a run to figure out *how* you run? In Chapter 1 we began to think about running differently, taking a new look at the forces at work. When our foot pushes down on the earth, the earth pushes back. There are all kinds of things that happen as we run that we simply don't realize because we never take the time to think about them. Maybe if we can become more conscious of what our bodies are doing we could use that knowledge to improve our running performance. The run is in fact a beautiful dance between the human body and the elements, driven by the cosmic beat of physics.

That's pretty poetic language to kick off a scientific discussion about running. It reflects a problem in running today. It seems every time you turn around, there's a new running style, form, or method coming out. Each one offers some revolutionary performance improvement, and all of them sound a little hokey. Some guy staggers out of the desert raving that he's learned the secrets of running from barefoot Indians. Another proclaims that to achieve running perfection you must become one with the universal spirit coursing through all sentient creatures. Their argument with each other is interrupted by the mad scientist who bursts in, shouting that his analysis of the moon landings proves that gravity can pull you forward as well as down.

Most athletes develop a healthy sense of skepticism of these characters in short order, and justifiably so. However, that doesn't mean these methods are entirely wrong. One of the biggest challenges facing today's running coaches is that a substantial amount of their knowledge is developed through personal experience. They have little background in scientific research. They are very knowledgeable and have many of the right answers, but they don't have the understanding of *why* they're right. It's like a person who memorizes multiplication tables without learning how to multiply.

This can be especially frustrating for triathletes, who are used to manufacturers explaining the science behind a product in excruciating detail. After investing thousands of dollars in a technologically advanced piece of equipment designed by computers to help your race performance, it's difficult to entrust the final leg of your race to a self-proclaimed guru. There is genuine science attached to the mechanics of running, and we will make it our goal to understand what it tells us about how we run.

Researchers have been studying the motion and forces of running for decades. Their findings represent a detailed understanding of human locomotion that frequently validates—and sometimes refutes—the proponents of various running methods. We can't cover everything those scientists have discovered in detail. Much of it delves into subjects that are of only marginal value to the competitive triathlete. We'll bypass that data and focus on the numbers that can make the most impact on your running.

You will come across a few unfamiliar equations and units of measurement in this chapter. It's perfectly reasonable to feel a little bewildered, but keep in mind that these concepts are primarily meant to serve as contextual references. If we arrive at an understanding of why the right answers are right, you'll be able to identify what things you can improve on. We'll start with our familiar foundation, the body and the medium.

THE MECHANICS OF RUNNING: THE BODY & THE MEDIUM

After leaving the bike in the transition area, we are back to the simpler form of the body once again, without additional equipment. Standing on your own two feet, you act as a large mass sitting on top of two multijointed, "spring-loaded" propulsion devices. The mass on top is, for the most part, irrelevant to the discussion. The legs, on the other hand, serve many functions: rigid support, flexible shock absorber, and force-generating lever system. They can perform more than one of these functions at a time, and frequently do throughout the running cycle.

Underneath and around the body we have earth and air, just as we did on the bike. The ground provides a force that holds you up and interacts with the soles of your feet so that you stay in one place without sliding out of control. The atmosphere once again presents challenges, but not in the same way it did on the bike. These are the fundamental components of running.

Push hard enough from a sitting position and you gradually overcome the force of gravity until your legs reach full extension and stop exerting muscular force. Then your bones take over and you stand. But what if you push a little harder? You accelerate more and stand faster. And if you push *really* hard? Liftoff! But how did you continue to move upward if your legs reached full extension and no longer stayed in contact with the ground? Simple. You reached a high enough velocity that momentum carried you upward in a hop or jump. Using Newton's laws, you turned yourself into an object in motion and tended to stay that way until a force acted upon you. Of course a force began acting on you. From the moment you took off from the ground, gravity began accelerating you back downward until your upward velocity turned into a downward one and you returned to the earth.

Running is best described as a series of one-legged hops in rapid succession. Your right foot pushes against the ground, and the ground pushes back. As you fall back to the ground, your left leg extends to break your fall and your left foot makes contact with the earth just long enough to push you back off again. In this moment, your right foot is halfway through its recovery motion and your right leg extends to again break your fall. The cycle is repeated as the ground pushes against you, again and again. This motion can be broken down into three primary phases:

Propulsion & liftoff: When you push off

Recovery: When you pick your leg up and extend it

Impact & braking: When gravity brings you back into contact with the ground and friction halts your forward motion

Scientists have developed highly sophisticated models to re-create this motion and a great deal of research has been done, extending far beyond the scope of what we want to accomplish here. What's important to understand is that your legs effectively act like springs throughout the running cycle. This notion can profoundly change how you run. "Tread lightly" takes on a whole new meaning when we start to consider the impact forces have on our performance.

With every strike of the foot, the earth will offer a force that is equal in magnitude and opposite in direction to the one exerted on it. We take a flying leap up and come down, take a leap and land, leap and land, and so on and so forth. This means that *the earth is exerting two vertical forces and two horizontal forces.* The best way to understand how all these forces act on us is with an easy summary: "There is nowhere to go but . . . " The earth does not push you forward. It does not push you up. Instead, *it works to prevent your foot from pushing downward or backward as you exert force.*

But when it comes to a sufficient amount of force, something's got to give. If the earth won't give way to your foot and move backward or downward, you'll just have to move onward and upward. We actually get where

THE TRIATHLETE VS. FORCES ON THE RUN

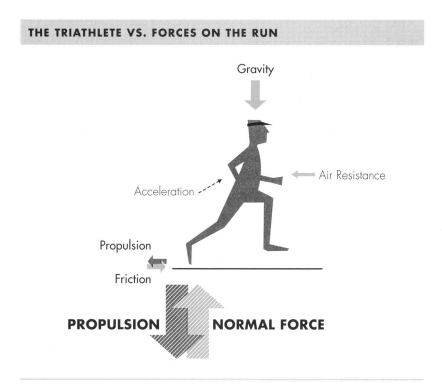

The athlete must produce enough force to accelerate upward and forward.

we want to go by losing a shoving match with the planet. Sometimes it pays to come in second place! This model also teaches us two very important things. Because the force your legs exert is downward and backward, our motion is a combination of a downward leg extension and a backward kick—with the earth pushing back to propel us forward.

If we break the forces down into their vertical and horizontal components, it becomes more clear. In the vertical direction, the earth exerts a normal force upward against us during the propulsion phase, equal to the force of our leg pushing downward. Because the ground does not give way, the force results in an upward acceleration of our body, giving us enough velocity to briefly achieve a very short flight. The second vertical force pushes up against us when we land (or impact), keeping us from crashing through the ground. This force is equal to the force generated by the acceleration of gravity acting on our mass. That's science-speak for "The bigger they are, the harder they fall." The direction of the vertical force doesn't change, but its *impact* on our running does. When we are leaping up, up, and away from earth, we gladly accept all the force it exerts. But when we come down, the upward force is in direct opposition to our downward trajectory. It's not such a happy reunion. Sound the collision alarm! And keep sounding it, because in a half-marathon the typical runner takes somewhere between 20,000 and 30,000 steps. Each one of those steps requires a propulsive and impact force.

The average runner will exert a force approximately equal to 2.5 times her body weight (force = mass multiplied by acceleration = weight) to push off the ground. As she comes back down, the impact force is about 1.6 times body weight.[1] Both of these forces occur in the quick span of time that your foot is on the ground, which is typically less than half a second. This means that a runner can experience anywhere between 275 and 750 pounds of force in a single step on level ground![2] There are obvious consequences for our joints, but we also have to consider the lateral forces at work.

If we only exerted a force in the vertical direction, there would be no acceleration and therefore no movement in the horizontal direction. So

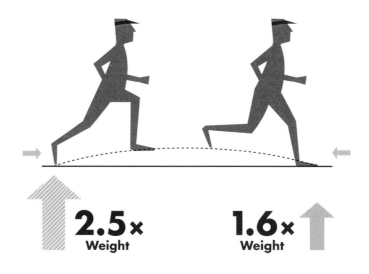

2.5× Weight   **1.6×** Weight

When running, your body experiences extraordinarily high forces proportionate to your body weight. The springlike nature of your muscles and the strength of your bones allow you to manage these forces.

we must conclude that some force is required, and thus exerted, in the horizontal direction when we run. That's the "kick" portion of the running movement. In the horizontal direction, the earth resists the backward motion of our foot as our muscles kick backward via the mechanism of friction. Once again, if the earth won't go in the direction we push it to go, we have to go the direction it pushes back against us. We move forward as we leap. As we land again there is a second, opposing force that resists the force attempting to drive our foot forward. The propulsive force of friction is approximately 30 percent of our body weight. It works against us at the same rate as our foot hits the ground, creating what is appropriately named the braking force.[3] This braking force is much appreciated, since without it we'd go sliding across the ground and probably wind up looking foolish.

Just like our bicycle tires pushing down against the road, our shoes encounter more friction as we increase the amount of weight on them. Once again, that friction force works both for and against us.

We run with one goal in mind: to propel our body toward the finish line. Along the way, our upper body makes a pitiful contribution to the running effort, instead serving primarily to sustain our vital organs and brain. As far as our legs are concerned, everything from the hips up is dead weight. The physical toll our joints and muscles pay is a direct reflection of how much mass we carry. With both their finishing times and long-term health at stake, every athlete is looking for the "right" way to run. All of the methods out there—ChiRunning, barefoot running, Pose Method, etc.—rely on the same fundamental concepts, which happen to be based on physics and lead to a singular objective: to make your legs the most efficient pogo sticks in the world.

POGO GADGET LEGS!: TUNING UP THE MECHANICS OF RUNNING ECONOMY

We run much the same way a pogo stick leaps around. A pogo stick bounces up and forward until it comes back to the ground, then it coils up and absorbs the impact. Coiling also prepares the stick to bounce up and forward again. During its flight, the lower portion of the stick swings forward so it's ready to catch us when it falls. When it leaps forward, the upper half of the pogo stick leads the way, and we have to swing the bottom forward to catch ourselves again. This means that while the stick is airborne, it moves very much like a pendulum, swinging from the back to the front. The bottom of the stick swings to the point that when it hits the ground, we're standing above it. If it were too far behind us, we'd fall on our faces, and if it were too far in front, we'd fall on our rears. There's a sweet spot for this point of impact, and it occurs approximately in front of a line that runs from the ground to our center of gravity.

Of these two movements, the springlike impact/propulsive movement and the swinging, pendulumlike movement, the impact/propulsive movement requires the most energy. In fact, the pendulum motion of a runner's legs is so small that it is not even considered in most research.[4] This further sharpens our new way of looking at running because it whittles away the less important elements so we can focus on the major performance factors. **The majority of the forces we experience during running occur in the vertical direction, not the lateral direction.** This means we spend more energy moving up and down than propelling ourselves forward.

It's almost as if we're saying that running is more about moving up and down than moving forward. In fact, that's *exactly* what science tells us. This leads us to a better understanding of running mechanics and efficiency. Although stride rate and stride length are important factors in developing running efficiency, science explains why all running methods boil down to achievement of an optimal lateral-to-vertical displacement ratio. In other words, we want to go the farthest distance forward in the least amount of distance up and down. Different running methods will tell you how to chase down this running nirvana, but science has a lot to say about it too.

There are three things we can change to increase the efficiency of our running mechanics:

- Reduce our vertical displacement

- Maximize the distance we cover per step

- Reduce the amount of time we spend in contact with the ground

By reducing our up-and-down motion, we will reduce the magnitude of the harmful impact force and the amount of effort we spend getting back in the air. Don't jump so high; don't land so hard—simple. Increasing our horizontal distance per step is equivalent to getting better gas mileage

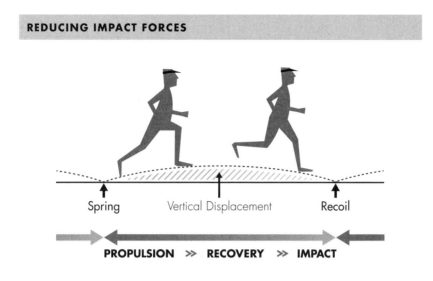

Spring Vertical Displacement Recoil

PROPULSION » RECOVERY » IMPACT

Because the springlike movement in running is the most costly, you need to run with minimal vertical displacement.

in our cars. The advantage of reducing the amount of time we spend in contact with the ground is a little less obvious.

In the most basic terms, the more time you spend in contact with the ground, the more time you spend landing, decelerating, accelerating, and taking off again. That adds up to more time spent experiencing forces on our legs and traveling at less than our maximum velocity. To increase speed, we want to be up in the air and flying, not going through security checks and taxiing on the runway! A stronger, bouncier spring (a.k.a. our muscles) will help us stay off the ground because a strong spring doesn't collapse as much as a weak one.

We can explore this principle further with a bouncy ball and a ball of clay. Drop them both on the ground and watch what happens. The clay doesn't bounce because it doesn't have the material strength to maintain its shape when forces act on it. The process by which it flattens on the bottom when it makes contact with the ground is called deformation. The bouncy ball does not deform as much and also regains its shape. The same goes for springs. More strength equals less deformation and better bouncing. To see this play out in real life, go to a local race and watch for the last runners struggling to reach the finish line. What does their running form look like? It's typically a very slow, shuffling movement, with as much time spent on the ground as off. They have very little propulsive power left, and they're really just striding forward as best they can. Watch closely and you'll see another consequence of their exhaustion. Their hips move up and down in a more exaggerated way because the same fatigue they are feeling in their legs prevents them from resisting the impact with the ground. Their springs are worn out, and as a result their hips sag.

Fixing problems of horizontal gain and vertical pain is somewhat complicated. Let's get a handle on them by revisiting our pogo stick analogy. Let's say you want to jump over a hole in the ground. Easy, right? Just bounce a little harder and your increased height gives you enough air time to make it to the other side. That's not what we want as runners, though. So how can we stay low and still get across? Just bounce lower and kick your stick forward more. Unfortunately, that also has a consequence. There's a limit to just how far we can kick out before we get into trouble. If the bottom of the stick (our leg) is too far in front of us when it hits the ground, then instead of following through and bouncing again, we wind up falling on our butt. We actually see this repeated frequently in the long jump during track-and-field competitions. The problem is that the landing point and our center of gravity are misaligned so much that forward momentum can't overcome the braking force the earth applies against us.

Scientists have found that the same case applies to running. Although going too far off the ground incurs one kind of energy waste, striding too far creates another costly expense. So we can neither reach an absolute minimum vertical displacement nor get a maximum horizontal distance. It's hopeless!

Not so fast. The idea was never to achieve *zero* vertical displacement or *infinite* horizontal distance. Rather, our goal is to reach the best efficiency. That means striking the perfect balance between the two. As it turns

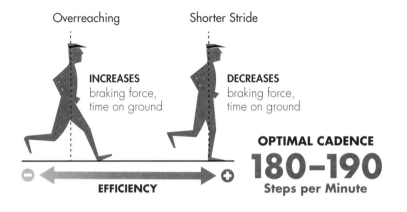

Overreaching | Shorter Stride

INCREASES braking force, time on ground

DECREASES braking force, time on ground

OPTIMAL CADENCE
180–190
Steps per Minute

EFFICIENCY

If your stride extends too far past your center of gravity, you will experience excessive braking force. This increases time on the ground and therefore the energy cost to maintain speed.

out, science indicates that an optimal solution does exist. It also resolves our spring stiffness problem. We can reduce our vertical displacement, increase distance, and decrease the time we spend on the ground, all in a single package!

And what is this magic solution that biomechanics researchers have discovered? It happens to be the same thing coaches have been telling triathletes for years: ***Shorten your stride and run at a cadence of 180–190 steps per minute.*** Now you have a better, scientific reason to believe this advice.

Without getting into the specifics of any of the branded methods of running, coaches all aim to change your running form from big, long strides to short, fast ones. What you lose in the amount of ground you cover in each stride you make up for by a reduction in waste: less wasted vertical force, less braking force resisting movement, and less time on the ground. Scientific studies of athletes have found the following benefits to reducing your stride and picking up the cadence:[5]

- 32 percent reduction of time spent in contact with the ground

- 76 percent reduction in total vertical displacement during the contact phase

- 100 percent increase in "spring stiffness"

These gains become even more important in light of studies on how the body's joints react to the propulsive and impact forces as a function of cadence and stride. Scientists measured the joint kinematics of several athletes running at constant speed while changing their stride and cadence. They discovered that forces on the ankle, knee, and hip were dramatically reduced when they increased their cadence by 10 percent of normal. When they slowed their cadence by 10 percent, the energy absorbed at all three points increased. This is a very important point for runners who have suffered injuries. A slow cadence can put undue stress on your joints.[6]

These findings are reinforced by studies that took the opposite approach. Instead of looking for the most efficient way to keep an athlete from burning energy, scientists observed how athletes' form changed as they ran to fatigue. What did they find? A progressively slower running cadence, more time spent in contact with the ground per step, and lower impact and propulsive forces.[7] In other words, their springs wore out. Analyzing the change in the force/time relationship produced another, more troubling conclusion: that a slow, shuffling run consumes more energy per step than the quicker, springier turnover of fresh legs.[8] The more tired you get, the more tired you *will* get. This is why pacing is so important in every phase of a triathlon. From the moment you get on the bike, you risk leg fatigue on the run.

It's important to remark that this is not an endorsement of any particular method or philosophy. There are as many running forms as there are marathon and triathlon winners. Winners' technique varies as much as their choice of footwear, but they all maintain a high cadence. How you do it isn't as important as how *long* you do it. A great technique is only great so long as it allows you to maintain your economy, and you want to be great all the way to the finish line. Things go downhill quickly from the moment your method fails you.

FROM KENYANS TO CLYDESDALES: THE UNKNOWN SCIENCE BEHIND RUNNING ECONOMY

It's a question often pondered by triathletes: What makes Kenyans so fast in the marathon? Patrick Makau currently holds the world record in the marathon at 2:03:38. He stands 5 feet 7 inches tall and weighs less than 130 pounds. Wouldn't a taller athlete be able to cover more ground per step, and therefore be more efficient over the course of 26.2 miles? That stands to reason, but how much ground a person can cover isn't the only measure of efficiency. Furthermore, the runners atop the podium typically aren't built like basketball players. What is it about diminutive runners that makes them so much better at distance running? It comes down to the physics of heat and energy. Being so much smaller, Makau requires less *effort* to push his body at a high speed for 26.2 miles. So while the basketball player can move his feet farther with each step, the Kenyan moves *easier*. Therefore, he can move faster while burning fewer calories, which helps him maintain a higher effort for a greater distance. That's not the whole story, though. The lighter athlete has a smaller *total* energy requirement, but you might be shocked to find out that, kilogram for kilogram, he's not substantially more efficient than a sumo wrestler. Physics moves in mysterious ways sometimes, and developing an appreciation for running economy requires us to wade through some weird science.

Regardless of athletic ability or the speed at which the athlete runs, scientists agree that a human being will expend the same amount of energy to run a given distance. That means you burn the same number of calories if you run a 6-minute mile, a 7-minute mile, or a 9-minute mile.

Measurements differ, and not every individual is the same, but the consensus is that your efficiency rate is somewhere between 0.85 and 1.00 kilocalories per kilogram of body mass per kilometer run.[9] This means that you will burn energy at a higher rate if you run faster, but you will also take less time to run the distance. So the "net burn" remains the same. The savvy triathlete who read the bike chapters might be skeptical at this point, and rightfully so. After all, it takes exponentially more power (and therefore more energy) to go faster on the bike, so why wouldn't the same hold true on the run?

The primary reason is that we don't run anywhere near as fast as we can ride on the bike, so aerodynamics doesn't factor into our running effort. But more relevant to the mechanics of running and our efforts to improve our running performance is how we burn those calories. Remember that the preponderance of our work goes into pushing our bodies up from the ground rather than driving them forward or swinging our legs along. That would lead us to conclude that a larger, heavier person has to do more work to push off the ground in order to cover the same distance. Let's make a quick calculation to compare. Obeying the energy burn rate of $E = 1$ kcal/kg/km, a 130-pound (59-kg) Kenyan only burns 59 kilocalories in a kilometer, while a 150-pound (68-kg) triathlete burns 68 kilocalories. Over a marathon distance, that equals a difference of 378 kilocalories, or 15 percent greater energy expenditure by the 150-pound triathlete. Remember, that's regardless of speed, so the triathlete comes up short on the efficiency scale whether it's in a training run or a race. However, the advantage of the Kenyan (or a smaller triathlete) goes beyond the energy required to simply move down the course. There's actually a much more important influence in this competition.

This is where science begins to get weird. There are strange proportions at work in the running mechanics of nearly every species on the planet. Scientific investigation into the physics of running began long ago with a person with whom we're already familiar: Galileo. He initially began by asking why there weren't giants on Earth. This may seem like an odd way to approach the subject of running economy, but in fact it's quite an effective starting point because our running efficiency is all about size. Through his research on the subject, Galileo came up with an area of physiological study that is known today as **scaling**. To understand how profoundly scaling impacts runners, let's start with a basic example of a cube.

Let's say our cube has sides that are 2 centimeters (0.02 m) long. Its area and volume are given by the following equations:[10]

Volume (length × width × height)

0.02 × 0.02 × 0.02 = 0.000008 m³

Area (number of sides × length × width)

6 × 0.02 × 0.02 = 0.0024 m²

Now let's suppose we double the cube's dimensions to 4 centimeters.

Volume = 0.000064 m³

Area = 0.0096 m²

Notice that the area increases by a factor of four, but the volume increases by a factor of *eight*. This turns out to be the case for any shape, and presents quite a problem for large animals. ***An animal's mass, relative skeletal strength, and energy consumption while running are all directly related to its size.*** Think of yourself as more or less made up of a consistent body mass, where any cubic centimeter of your body has the same density as any other cubic centimeter. That being the general case, it means that even a small increase in your body's size (be it height or girth) incurs a serious weight penalty. This is why giants are few and far between: If an animal were to increase proportionately in size, its bones would only become four times as big around while its weight would increase by a factor of eight. The larger body would weigh so much that the bones would not be strong enough to support the load. Elephants don't typically gallop because their bones are almost maxed out supporting their weight in standing and walking. The best they can manage is their "race walk" when they charge. Excessive propulsive and impact forces resulting from long-duration up-and-down motion would damage their joints or possibly break a bone. At the other end of the scale, animals such as dogs, cats, and rodents use bounding strides to run. In the context of large- and small-animal gaits, a human's mass-to-skeletal strength ratio allows for a running form somewhere in between. We exist in a happy medium—happier, in fact, than what most animals enjoy. *Human beings enjoy several advantages over other animals in terms of running performance thanks to our mass.* We are more efficient than most smaller animals on the planet, and our total energy requirement to run a given distance allows us to endure longer distances than most larger animals can. We are also well-proportioned to withstand the impact forces experienced when moving fast.

It's not just our bone strength that scales proportionately to our size. Between species, the amount of energy required to run also follows a fairly strict mathematical relationship. Scientists have determined that mathematical relationship to be proportionate to:

$$E_{run} = m^{-0.33}$$

Where E_{run} is the amount of oxygen required to move 1 kilogram of body mass 1 kilometer (kJ/kg/km), and m is the mass of the animal.

It's worth noting that physicists use kilometers when measuring E_{run} instead of minutes. So this isn't the same as VO_2, but it's a close cousin.

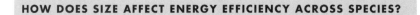

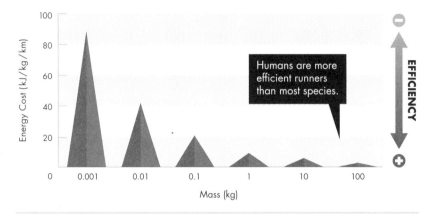

Humans burn 0.85–1.00 kilocalories per kilogram of body mass to run 1 kilometer. We are more efficient than smaller species, and we have a lower net energy cost than larger animals.

From one species to another, efficiency of movement increases as the animal gets larger. This is primarily because smaller animals have to take more steps per kilometer, and therefore have to undergo those energy-sucking up-and-down motions more times. Human beings break this rule slightly because of the fact that we're one of the few animals on the planet that runs on two legs. However, we're still more efficient than most animals smaller than a midsized dog. As for animals that are larger and more efficient than us, we have another advantage. Consider a race between a man and a horse. Horses can obviously get around the track at the Kentucky Derby faster than any Olympic sprinter, but they lose out to humans in the ultra-marathon.[11] Although they are energetically more efficient, they still require substantially more net energy to cover the same distance because of their greater size. And now you have a scientific explanation for the old saying "hungry as a horse"!

There is a necessary caveat to make at this point. You may remember back to the beginning of this section when we said that the basketball player is *not* more efficient than the Kenyan because of his size. So how can an animal like a horse be more efficient than a human because of its size, but a larger human is less efficient than a smaller human? The contradiction is explained by the fact that basketball players and Kenyans are from the same species, but horses and people are not. The morphological differences between humans and other animals is generally so extreme that their differing size and stride length are the overwhelming factors in determining running performance. And, people run upright, which skews results slightly. But when you compare two humans to each other, the difference in aerobic efficiency is so narrow that several other factors (training, metabolism, other genetic differences, etc.) can influence them. The formula on page 131 only works when we compare distinct species.

Scaling dictates the terms of running performance in humans and every other running animal on the planet in another important way. Remember the earlier discussion that the majority of running forces occur in the vertical direction, and that all animals essentially take successive leaps to run. Because of that trend, the amount of energy we expend to run is dependent on the effort we spend on vertical displacement. The energy required to make that vertical displacement is defined as:

$$E_{vert} = mgh$$

*Where **m** is mass, **g** is gravity, and **h** is vertical distance (height).*

Based on observations of the motion of different species, scientists have established that the rate of energy consumption required to move one body length in a single step is approximately the same for all animals. It is roughly expressed as:

$$E_L = 0.75 \text{ J/kg}$$

*Where **J** = X, and **kg** = kilograms.*[12]

It seems as though we're comparing apples to oranges by looking at energy in the vertical and horizontal directions. However, this leads to an incredible revelation. Remember, the majority of our energy expenditure happens in the vertical plane. Yet we know from observation how much energy it takes us to cover one body length in a single step. This gives us the numerical values for every element of the equations on page 133 except height. Using a little algebra, we come up with an interesting ratio for just about every running animal on earth, and perhaps the most potent rule for triathletes on the run: *A runner has to leap 7.5 centimeters in the air in order to cover one body length.*[13]

This is quite a discovery, because it gives a fairly accurate gauge for judging running form. Running coaches often discuss "flattening" a stride or tell runners not to bounce so much. Now we understand the physical reason why. When we don't maximize the horizontal distance we cover as it relates to the amount of effort we make to leave the ground, we are running in a highly inefficient manner. The 7.5-centimeter rule is a good starting point. It becomes even more important when you consider a runner's natural selection of stride length. Our stride length typically doesn't equal our full height until we're in a dead sprint.[14] A well-trained marathoner will select a stride length that is somewhere between 75 and 90 percent of her total height. This means that she has less of a vertical displacement requirement.

Just to be clear, this is not a directive to go stick rulers in your yard at odd intervals and make camera phone videos of yourself running past them to analyze your running form. But if you look at a ruler to see what 7.5 centimeters looks like, on your next run you might be able to learn something about your stride.

Running coaches have long told athletes to focus on optimizing their stride because doing so accomplishes several things at once. It's proven more difficult for coaches to relate the "what" of high cadence and optimal stride length to the "how" of improved running economy. For years, articles and magazines have described running economy in terms of reduced oxygen uptake. That's good, but it only left us with another mystery to explain. Science tells us that high cadence and adjusted stride length have never been the solution to running economy. They are simply the means to achieve the solution. *What really makes us better runners is reducing vertical forces and vertical energy expenditure while maximizing horizontal velocity.*

This makes a significant contribution to the Kenyans' success in the marathon. The taller runner does gain a slight distance advantage with his longer legs, but he pays a much greater penalty with the increased weight that comes as a consequence. Size does matter, but it's all about the scale of things.[15] However, it's about more than the energy required to move down the road. Once again, we have to contend with the air around us. But this time the atmosphere puts a new twist on its effort to resist us. The biggest advantage smaller athletes have on the run is how they manage the heat.

THE BIG NOT-SO-EASY: HEAT DISSIPATION VERSUS ATHLETE SIZE

Our introduction to the principle of scaling using a cube as an example revealed that the amount of volume and mass of an object increase at a much greater rate than its surface area. This has an indirect yet profound impact on running ability. Again, studies and measurements have allowed scientists to develop a scaling factor for the amount of skin area of an animal based on its mass.[16] The relationship is:

Skin Area $= 0.1 \text{ m}^{0.67}$

At the same time, there's also a scaling factor for the amount of heat your body generates as a function of mass. It is expressed as:

$$\textit{Heat (Watts)} = mv \times 4 \; \frac{J}{kg \times m}$$

*Where **m** is the mass of the runner, **v** is the runner's speed in meters per second, and $4 \frac{J}{kg \times m}$ is the scaling factor for determining heat.[17]*

Let's stop here and get a comparative feel for how this starts to influence running performance. We'll take three hypothetical athletes. Our first is a 121-pound (55-kg) elite Kenyan marathoner. Our second candidate is a more American/European-sized 132-pound (60-kg) professional runner. Our third candidate is a 165-pound (75-kg) age grouper. Height does not have to be the same because the physical relationships of mass and surface area remain constant regardless of morphology. All of our athletes are male, since most studies on heat production and dissipation involve runners of the same gender. (Furthermore, most studies involving women are specifically meant to determine differences with respect to gender, making extrapolation of the equations here more difficult.) Let's put our runners on the start line and have them jog off at a leisurely 6-minute mile (4.47 m/sec) pace. What is their relative heat production?

	KENYAN RUNNER	PRO RUNNER	AGE GROUPER
Mass	55 kg	60 kg	75 kg
Surface Area	1.47 m^2	1.55 m^2	1.80 m^2
Heat Production	983 W	1,073 W	1,341 W

Initially, it looks like things are pretty even. Though the amateur triathlete creates an extra 358 watts of heat as compared to the elite Kenyan runner, he also has an extra three and a half square feet of surface area to vent it. The sad reality of the situation is that the heat gets turned up with every extra gram of mass and inch of speed. Watch what happens when we tell our runners to gradually pick up the pace.

Not only does the athlete with greater mass (again, this can either be due to extra weight or simply a result of being taller) start out generating more heat, but his rate of heat generation increases more quickly than the

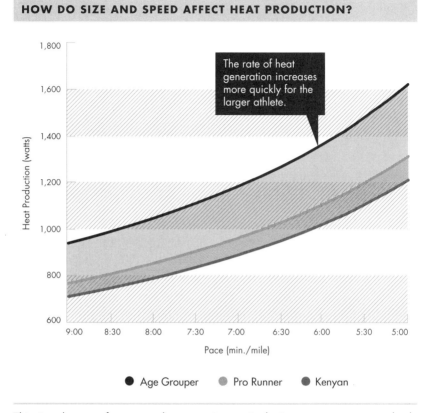

The rate of heat generation increases more quickly for the larger athlete.

● Age Grouper ● Pro Runner ● Kenyan

This is where surface area becomes increasingly important—can your body expel heat at a rate that keeps up with production? Athletes with greater mass will have a much harder time.

smaller athlete's.[18] This in itself does not necessarily represent a problem for the athlete of greater mass if he can expel heat at a rate that keeps up with its production. That's where surface area really comes into play, and also, unfortunately, where problems are compounded for the athlete of greater mass.

There are three primary forms of heat loss for an athlete on the run: convection, radiation, and evaporation. **Convection** is the transfer of heat through the movement of fluid currents across solid mediums of different temperatures. That's a fancy physics way of saying hot radiators make cold air hot, and cold air blowing across your skin carries heat away from you. Thermal **radiation** is the emission of thermal energy. Instead of the heat being carried away by air, it leaves the body in the form of electromagnetic energy. Think of the infrared cameras in night vision devices used by the military. Those cameras are able to see objects because the cameras are specially designed to detect the heat energy emitted by objects. We don't see this energy, because our eyes can only detect radiation in the visible light spectrum, but there are cases when you can observe it with the naked eye. Consider a piece of metal left in the fire until it gets red hot. The metal is so hot that some of the heat is actually radiated as light. The body works the same way, though at a much lower level. Finally, the form of heat transfer we're most familiar with is evaporation. **Evaporation** is the process by which a liquid is transformed into a vapor. In our case, we are mostly concerned with water. Water changes from a liquid to a gas as it absorbs heat energy and reaches a more excited state. Water gathers on our bodies as we perspire, and literally carries the heat away with it as energy as it turns into a vapor and floats away from our bodies.

The surface area of a human body affects how much heat can be transferred away. The rate of heat loss due to convection for a human being is calculated by:

$$C = (T_{skin} - T_{ambient}) \times A^2 \times 8.3 \times \sqrt{v}$$

*Where **C** is the convection rate in watts, **T_{skin}** is the skin surface temperature, **$T_{ambient}$** is the ambient air temperature, **A** is the surface area of the body, and **v** is velocity in meters per second.*

Heat loss due to radiation is given by:

$$R = (T_{skin} - T_{ambient}) \times A^2 \times 5.2$$

*Where **R** is the rate at which heat is radiated, **T_{skin}** is the skin surface temperature, and **$T_{ambient}$** is the ambient air temperature.*

Heat loss due to evaporation is calculated by:

$$E = (P_{sk} - P_a) \times A^2 \times 124 \times \sqrt{v}$$

Where E is the rate of heat loss due to evaporation measured in watts, and $(P_{sk} - P_a)$ is the difference in water vapor pressure as measured next to the skin and in the ambient air.

The atmospheric terms add complexity to the estimate of an athlete's heat exchange rate on any given day, but the math confirms what's already intuitive to us: The hotter it gets, the more difficult it becomes to shed heat. Think of the atmosphere around you as if it were a suitcase that holds heat. It can only hold so much; the fuller it gets, the more difficult it becomes to stuff more into it. The same holds true for humidity. The air can only hold so much water vapor. If it reaches its maximum capacity, there's nowhere for your sweat to go, and it will tend to stay on your skin regardless of how hot you get.

For two athletes running the same race in the same conditions, the difference in their performance will be determined by the variables of surface area and speed. Assuming an outdoor temperature of 95 degrees Fahrenheit and a relative humidity of 60 percent, let's graph the total heat dissipation of our lightest and heaviest runners, then compare it to the rate at which they generate heat.

The lighter athlete has a distinct advantage in terms of heat exchange. He can run at a nearly 6-minute mile pace before he begins to overheat, whereas the 165-pound (75-kg) athlete starts accumulating heat at the 9-minute mile mark. However, it's necessary to remark that science doesn't have the final say at this point. Many a 150-pound man has run a superb marathon time, and Kenyans have been beaten by American and European professionals on very hot days. Pain tolerance, competitive determination, and several physiological X factors yet to be understood by science play a part in a race's outcome. Just because the runner begins loading up on heat doesn't mean that he will immediately suffer consequences. However, once heat begins to accumulate, it will begin to work against an athlete. To increase its heat dissipation, the body will direct more blood to the skin, thus taking it away from the muscles. The added cardiovascular demand causes an increase in heart rate. An athlete reaches his maximum VO_2 at a slower pace when running in warmer temperatures. Indeed, both statistical analysis of actual race performances and controlled experiments involving elite marathoners have shown a direct correlation between an

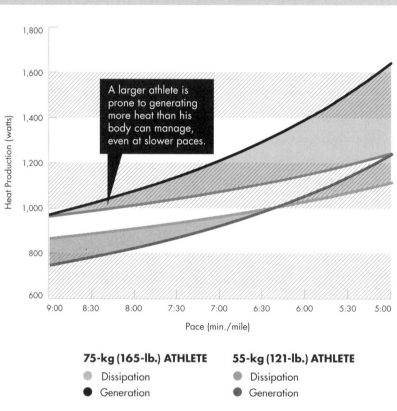

HOW DO SIZE AND SPEED AFFECT HEAT DISSIPATION?

A larger athlete is prone to generating more heat than his body can manage, even at slower paces.

Heat Production (watts)

Pace (min./mile)

75-kg (165-lb.) ATHLETE
- Dissipation
- Generation

55-kg (121-lb.) ATHLETE
- Dissipation
- Generation

In this scenario, our hypothetical athletes are running on a hot day (95 degrees) with moderate humidity (60 percent).

athlete's mass and his running performance in different temperatures.[19] The bottom line is that nature dictates your mass and surface area to an extent according to your height and skeletal structure, but you still have the ability to significantly improve on what nature gave you. *Shedding unnecessary pounds yields performance benefits that extend beyond lightening the load you carry on the course. It will also change the relative rate at which your body generates and expels heat, tipping the scales toward a faster run time.*

Between the effects of air resistance and air temperature on athletes throughout a race and the distinct differences in energy requirements and heat dissipation for athletes based on size, physics rewards certain body types in different categories. This is a strong justification of the Clydesdale and Athena divisions in races. Those gender-based weight divisions were created because even an extremely well-conditioned athlete taking up triathlon will be at a disadvantage if his or her mass is at the high end of the bell curve. All the athleticism in the world can't overcome the physical limitations of mass and energy. These weight-based categories are not for fat people, as some might assume. A fit, lean basketball player faces the same challenges as an untrained average-height person with unhealthy body weight. Naturally, if muscles makes up a higher percentage of his mass, he is better equipped to meet those challenges.

DON'T STAND SO CLOSE TO ME: CAN YOU REALLY DRAFT ON THE RUN?

We've discussed the benefits of drafting on the swim, and the advantage of drafting on the bike is so well understood that the practice has been rendered illegal in most races. But what about on the run? What role does aerodynamics play in the final phase of a triathlon, and is there a reason to follow closely behind the competition? As with any other form of terrestrial travel, aerodynamics does in fact play a role in running performance.

Indeed, the first generation of aerodynamic garments worn during the time trials of the Tour de France had their origins in Nike's research to make faster threads for the 2000 Olympic Games in Sydney, Australia.[20] Research on aerodynamics in running goes as far back as the 1970s, though much of the science is still difficult to verify. The problem facing researchers is the extremely dynamic nature of runners. Not only do their arms move as much as their legs, but there is a great deal of vertical motion in their entire body as opposed to that of a cyclist or swimmer. Still, given the conditions of the run phase of any triathlon, research is still able to provide an answer to the drafting question.

The answer is that drafting does work in a runner's favor, but only if you're a world-class athlete running in an Olympic distance triathlon. If you can run at a speed close to 11 mph (18 kph) (a 5:20 pace per mile/3:30 pace per kilometer), then sneaking into the aerodynamic shadow of a leader would ostensibly save you about a minute over the entire 10K run course. However, that doesn't account for the fact that you'd have to come out of the shadow if you want to take first, and you are betting on your competitor's ability to maintain that pace without drafting somebody else. So while it works on a scientific level, it's a more dubious proposition for actual racing.[21] Mathematical models predict that you begin picking up an aerodynamic advantage once you close to within 2 meters of the runner in front of you. *Wind tunnel tests suggest that the optimal distance is 1 meter, at which point you will experience a drag force that is only 37 percent as strong as that of the runner in front of you.*[22] For world-class athletes competing in the 1,500-meter event, this is equivalent to a 4-second advantage. Any closer, and your advantage dissipates rapidly, not to mention that you'll most likely irritate your leader.

Of course, 11 mph is hardly what the average age-group triathlete will accomplish in an Olympic distance triathlon, let alone an Ironman. So unless you're already at the front of a hotly contested pack moving at a furious pace, the question of whether you should try to pass someone or sneak into their draft zone may be a moot point. The other qualification concerns how precise you have to be with your drafting for it to be effective. Wind tunnel tests indicate that if you stray too far from being directly behind someone, the draft advantage falls off sharply. In testing, subjects who ran alongside each other actually experienced an overall *increase* in drag.[23] While no detailed explanation has been investigated, the combined surface area of the two runners appears to work cumulatively against both of them. It's possible that a runner would experience more than 25 percent extra drag running side by side with another runner than if he ran alone.[24] Again, this all occurs at very fast speeds. Even if you turn 6-minute splits, it doesn't apply to you.

A DISCUSSION WORTH REPEATING: RUNNING ON HILLS

We've already discussed the impact hills have on triathletes during the bike phase. And the odds are pretty good that if you tackled serious hills on the bike course, you'll see a few more between T2 and the finish line. Running is a significantly different mode of travel than cycling, however, so we can expect that terrain will take its toll on runners in a unique way.

Just exactly how it affects you depends on how you want to look at it. In cycling, the only real way to assess the impact of hills is by knowing how they affect an athlete's speed for a given power output. Only when you know the power requirement can you correlate your physical response to geography's demands. In running, the relationship between speed and physiology is more direct. Instead of having to go through bicycle cranks to transfer power, you apply your legs directly to the road. This makes it more convenient to understand the price we pay to get over the hill. It comes down to a simple choice. Do you want to go slower or work harder? Your answer may depend on *how much* harder you have to work, so let's get a handle on the costs and benefits.

There have not been many scientific studies on the specific phenomenon of an incline's impact on running performance, but those that have been conducted have closely replicated the other studies' results and agree on the trends they indicate. The indication provides us with a new rule of thumb for running. *For every 1 percent increase in the grade of a hill, a runner will either increase his VO$_2$ by 2.6 mL/kg/min or reduce his speed by 0.82 kilometers per hour (kph).*[25]

Even with a precise understanding of heart rate and how it correlates to your VO$_2$, you'd still need to memorize the topography of the run course (or use an inclinometer on your GPS watch) to really make use of the knowledge of how an incline increases your oxygen uptake. And hopefully you'll be running hard enough that you can't recall the necessary information or do the math on it! It would probably be more helpful to look at things in a more intuitive way. Let's first assume that you are in fact running at a hard pace on a race course. If you are wearing a heart rate monitor, you are trying to stay within a certain limit to avoid hitting the wall. From your training, you know that an increase in heart rate corresponds to a certain speed over the familiar terrain you usually run during training. But what if this is an Ironman 70.3 course halfway across the country and you suddenly encounter some hills that didn't look so big on the course map? It would be nice if you could adjust your pace early on so that your heart rate doesn't go through the roof. Then you wouldn't have to slow down too much only to find out your pace on the ascent is slower than you could have managed. Hitting a hill like this can cause a runner to go through a yo-yo progression of slowing down and speeding up several times, costing both time and unwanted burn in the legs. Can that initial judgment call at the base of the hill can be made in a more informed way? A pace of 0.82 kilometers per hour doesn't mean a whole lot, and it doesn't convert neatly into minutes per mile. The graph on page 145 shows how increasing slope affects an athlete's pace based on what an athlete's typical pace would be on level ground. Find the line that best fits your speed on flat roads and trace along it to get a general indicator of how you might want to approach hills. Keep in mind that these lines represent a constant effort, so every athlete will have different curves for workouts of varying intensity. Also remember that this is a guideline. There are many runners out there who train on hills or are simply better adapted to them. But if you're training for a mountain marathon and don't have a lot of hills nearby, this will give you a good starting reference.

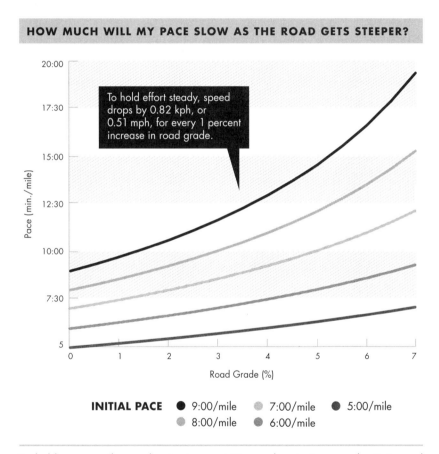

HOW MUCH WILL MY PACE SLOW AS THE ROAD GETS STEEPER?

To hold effort steady, speed drops by 0.82 kph, or 0.51 mph, for every 1 percent increase in road grade.

Pace (min./mile)

Road Grade (%)

INITIAL PACE ● 9:00/mile ○ 7:00/mile ● 5:00/mile
○ 8:00/mile ● 6:00/mile

To hold pace as the road gets steeper, VO_2max has to increase by 2.6 mmol for every additional 1 percent increase in road grade. It's best to choose those redline efforts carefully unless you're near the end of your race.

HERMES' SANDALS: WHAT'S TO BE GAINED FROM LIGHTER SHOES, SHORTS & SHIRTS

Shoe manufacturers have advertised advances in material and fabrication technologies since the first Nike "waffle runners" appeared in the 1970s. Even today, new designs consistently break with conventions and set the bar even higher in different performance areas. In some ways the top-of-the-line models from every manufacturer are very close to each other. In other ways, they are quite distinct. Athletes have strong preferences for intangible aspects like fit and feel. This begs the question, Does a lighter shoe really provide a performance boost, and how great is the relative advantage?

Scientists have researched this matter in great detail, and they have found that lightening the runner's load has its advantages. Multiple studies demonstrate a strong correlation between the amount of weight attached to the lower limbs and an increase in aerobic demand. *Oxygen demand increases somewhere between 5 and 10 percent for every kilogram of extra mass below the knee.*[26]

The range of uncertainty in the increase is based on the fact that the studies did not exactly replicate the method for adding weight to the legs and feet of the test subjects. The results are nonetheless significant. However, a kilogram is also a significant amount of weight, and no one wears shoes that heavy. In recent years shoes from brands popular among triathletes show a much lighter spectrum of applied mass.

SHOE	WEIGHT
Newton MV²	5.8 oz. (164 g)[27]
Nike Flyknit	5.6 oz. (160 g)[28]
Zoot ULTRA Race 3.0	8.9 oz. (252 g)[29]
Adidas BOOST	9.6 oz. (272 g)[30]
K-Swiss Kwicky Blade-light N	9.0 oz. (255 g)[31]

So it can be reasonably assumed that triathletes are running with less than 275 grams strapped to their feet. Research has established that the relationship between mass and aerobic cost is linear, and therefore a quarter of the weight only incurs a quarter as much penalty.[32] Any shoe 275 grams or less should only increase your aerobic demand between 1.25 and 2.5 percent compared to running with no shoes at all. Of course, the real takeaway is that with only 112 grams of difference between the "heavy" Adidas shoe and the "ultra light" Nike, you save slightly more than 1 percent aerobic performance. That may matter a great deal to world-class athletes, but the rest of us are probably more concerned with getting a shoe in our favorite color.

This might get you thinking about the rest of the gear you use in racing and training. Don't sweat it. The aerobic weight penalty doesn't work the same on the torso as it does on the legs. Theoretical and experimental results disagree, but nothing suggests your nutrition is doing you more harm than good. An extra kilogram around the waist increases oxygen demand by 0.5 percent.[33] Your hydration bottle belt, the extra gels in your pocket, your heart rate monitor, sunglasses, visor, and watch aren't going to make a noticeable impact on your run. Given that, it's hardly worth troubling yourself over a lighter pair of shorts or top. So if weight isn't a huge factor in performance, one may begin to wonder if a *heavier* shoe is advantageous. In the effort to reduce shoe mass, what's been shaved off most over time is the rubber underneath. That same material is often advertised as providing "energy return." Have "advancements" in shoe technology been going the wrong way this whole time, or is there a balance between cushioning and weight?

KICKS & THE CITY: IS YOUR SOLE MATE OUT THERE?

Besides a shoe's weight, the aspect of its design most often discussed by manufacturers is the sole. The two primary factors you hear in advertising are cushioning and energy return. Oddly, few companies try to compete on the durability front. Instead, they generally agree that you should change your shoes every 400–500 miles.

When you think about it, all of this seems a little confusing. Why is it that a shoe with superior cushioning and/or energy return doesn't last longer than its competitors? If it "bounces back" better from each individual impact with the ground, wouldn't the same principle apply over a cumulative distance? And while we're on the subject, how exactly do we quantify things like cushioning and energy return? For all the tests and simulations that bike manufacturers run to prove the superiority of their designs, wouldn't a shoe maker benefit by presenting conclusive proof that their shoes give you the most bounce for your buck? Why not just come out with a credible scientific report showing the material properties of a shoe instead of inventing nonsense terms that have no real meaning?

The simple answer is that "Exotech Nitrospeed" sounds a lot cooler than ethylene vinyl acetate or thermoplastic polyurethane. Those are two of the most widely used materials in your shoes, and in addition to not sounding cool, their names really don't tell you much about the shoe's quality unless you're a chemical engineer. Further complicating the issue is that **the architecture of the shoe's construction is just as important as its material**. Consequently, even if we narrow the selection to each manufacturer's top-of-the-line models, it's nearly impossible to compare all the available shoes on the market in meaningful ways. Add in the constant design changes that occur every year, and it seems like a total roll of the dice. But all is not lost. Just as in bicycle design, manufacturers who disagree on design nuances are still guided by fundamental principles. Knowing those principles gives the smart triathlete a few more parameters to help them make a wise decision.

Let's first consider how scientists measure cushioning and energy return. To be as accurate as possible in measuring a shoe's material properties, they use a special machine that resembles a jackhammer with sensors on it. The shoe is attached to a table and then the jackhammer hits it with a force that approximates a runner's foot impacting the ground. Scientists then look for two specific moments in the impact cycle. The first moment comes just after the "foot" hits the ground. In a span of milliseconds, your foot mashes down into the shoe's sole, squashing the foam and rubber underneath. The farther the foot mashes down, the more resistance the sole puts up. That resisting point reaches its peak at the point when the sole finally stops the foot's downward motion. While most runners will never know exactly when this occurs, the machinery detects it easily. The peak force is used as the measure of a shoe's cushioning. The *lower* the magnitude of this peak force, the better the cushioning is.[34]

The second moment comes as the jackhammer is allowed to bounce off the shoe. Scientists measure the maximum height the hammer reaches after hitting the shoe, then use that measurement, combined with the hammer's mass and the height from which it was dropped, to determine how much of the impact energy was returned.[35] One might be led to imagine jumping onto a water bed or a mattress with springs. The water bed has great cushioning, but doesn't give you much bounce. The spring mattress is less comfortable, but you get more bounce. So you'd think that shoes work the same way. Aha! There's a tradeoff between cushioning and energy return. Now we're getting somewhere!

Unfortunately, and much to the triathlete's aggravation, shoes don't work that way. First, the physical properties of those unglamorously named materials allow them to absorb impact and return energy without trading one for the other. While this is overall a good thing for shoes, it still leaves relative advantages between specific models shrouded in mystery. And again, there are the differences in the actual shape of the sole, meaning that two shoes made of the same material aren't equal. It's like there's just too much variation to really know the difference.

Eureka! That's exactly it! The most important thing to know is that there's no way to know! ***There is no magic combination of material composition and structural assembly that makes one shoe really better than another.*** In fact, independent tests of shoes of varying prices and brands found surprising results. Subjects were asked to run on a treadmill and assess the relative comfort of the shoe. Researchers simultaneously measured the impact forces within the shoes. There was no correlation between brand, price, cushioning, or "comfort" assessment.[36] Another study focused on differences in actual shoe design by selecting shoes with soles made of the same material (ethylene vinyl acetate), but with different sole structures. While lab tests showed significant differences between the shoes in terms of cushioning and energy return, measurements of test subjects actually running in them found no change in running performance, form, or interactions with the ground during impact. The researchers concluded that while a shoe might win in the lab, it doesn't perform noticeably better on the road.[37] Furthermore, whether manufacturers make a shoe more or less expensive, differences in shoe design don't necessarily make them better. Just because a shoe has higher energy return doesn't necessarily mean it benefits you. Studies have found that even shoes with superior energy return as measured in laboratory conditions do not seem to give athletes a measurable benefit during actual running.[38] It is possible that the design of the shoe can cause it to return energy in the wrong direction or at the wrong time.[39]

This revelation becomes especially helpful when you look at how shoes perform over the long term. Results of studies on the durability of running shoes indicate that, regardless of the material composition or construction, *cushioning and energy return both degrade about 3–5 percent after the first 200–300 miles of wear and continue to do so as the miles pile up.*[40] And considering how quickly they pile up for a serious runner, you could find yourself making a trip to the shoe store every three to four months. It's even worse for professional marathoners like Ryan Hall, who runs 100 miles a week and changes out his shoes twice a month.[41] Notably, his sponsoring shoe company doesn't protest. This material degradation in running shoes is no mystery to the shoe manufacturers, which is why they have never tried to promote a line of shoes for its resilience.

What happens as a shoe begins to lose its bounce remains somewhat ambiguous, though scientists have established trends. Indications are that we gradually adapt our running form to the changes in the shoe—and not in a good way. Peak impact forces appear to increase due to the loss of cushioning, but the foot appears to remain in contact with the ground for a longer period of time. Both of these are indicators of reduced performance. Changes in overall posture and whole-body motion have also been observed, but their effects are unknown.[42]

At the end of the day, there is really no difference in the performance of modern running shoes. Lighter or heavier, more or less material on the sole, more or less expensive. The models advertised to be at the top of the line hold only marginal, if any, advantage over their mid-range cousins. The best advice for optimal performance is to set aside your favorite shoes for racing and find a comfortable model in the bargain bin for training. You're more likely to prevent injury and maintain good training form by swapping out cheap shoes frequently than staying in a "good" pair for a long time. But while shoes can't change the running game, they are only half the running equation. Let's briefly examine the turns physics can take when you exit the well-worn paths and paved roads.

THE ROAD LESS TRAVELED: HOW TREADMILLS, TRAILS & BEACHES AFFECT YOUR RUN

If you're close enough to a shoreline, nothing beats a run along the beach. And even if you're in a landlocked region, there's always a scenic trail out there waiting to be discovered. Running is supposed to be liberating, physically empowering, something to help clear the mind. So why restrict yourself to the encumbrances of crosswalks, stoplights, and sidewalks as you train for a triathlon? Get *out* there.

Just go with an understanding of what you're getting *into*.

Pretty much all standard modern footwear is built for walking on pavement and concrete. We evolved hard surfaces to facilitate the motion of wheeled vehicles, which in turn required us to evolve our shoes to facilitate walking on hard surfaces. That doesn't mean your street shoes can't function as trail runners, but it does mean that most human beings are more used to running where the interaction between their feet and the pave-ment is very different from the interaction between their feet and a natural surface. So what changes when the urban athlete starts bounding along the grass, dirt, creeks, beaches, and rocky ravines of the undiscovered country? Energetically speaking, quite a bit.

As one might expect, natural surfaces do a much better job of absorb-ing impact forces. In tests comparing the influence of different surfaces on running economy, scientists placed a force measurement plate on the ground and measured the impact force under different terrain conditions. The control condition was the uncovered hard surface, and test coverings were constructed for grass and sandy environments. The reductions in peak impact deceleration force were astounding. There was a 92 percent reduc-tion in force on the grassy surface, 93 percent reduction on wet sand, and 98 percent reduction on soft, dry sand.[43] That's some serious cushioning.

That softer ride comes with a price, however. A comparison of stud-ies showed the following increases in energy cost, and therefore VO_2, as a result of running on softer surfaces.[44]

SURFACE	ENERGY COST
Hard Surface	---
Sand	63%
Grass	4.9%
Treadmill	−11%

It's interesting to note that four different experiments found the simi-lar result that it is actually *easier* to run on a treadmill from an energy cost perspective.[45] This measurement only accounts for the energy return provided by the surface. On top of that, there is also no air resistance because you don't actually move forward. Studies show that to incur an effort level that simulates running forward as you normally would, the treadmill must be set at a 1 percent incline from the beginning.[46] However, given the findings above, it would have to be set even higher to account for the energetic gain in the surface energy return. Just keep that in mind the next time you turn a marathon personal record on the treadmill and start thinking you might do just as well come race season. You could be setting yourself up with some unrealistic expectations.

And now, as they say, we have run our course. We have addressed the primary issues of physics and human locomotion. If everything has gone well for you in your race, you've hit the finish line by this point. What's left to discuss? A lot, actually. What's the first thing just about every triathlete does as soon as they cross the finish line? They look at their watch. Fifteen minutes after emerging victorious from another successful battle with the universe, with pizza and beer in hand, the process starts all over again. The discussions with fellow athletes begin. The mental replay starts, an internal commentary breaks the whole thing down, moment by moment. There's a memory of a slip in transition here, an ill-advised surge on the bike there, and a little mental math tallying the seconds all those mistakes cost. By the time they're loading the bike onto the back of their car, the analysis is clear: "I could've done that faster."

That's the addicting part of triathlon: the constant competition with self. And while much of your performance depends on how well you perform in the three disciplines, there is also the "fourth discipline" of race strategy. There, too, science has a few tips to help the savvy triathlete shave time off her finish line appearance. So we're not done yet after all. Let's pull it all together and make a smart swimmer, runner, and cyclist into a faster triathlete!

CHAPTER 6

A SCIENTIFIC APPROACH TO RACING STRATEGY

FINDING YOUR HAPPILY EVER AFTER: LOOKING AT THE RACE FROM START TO FINISH

We've now covered the scientific principles involved with every discipline of triathlon. Just as with the typical triathlon race, we ended on the run. And yet for all that's been discussed in terms of science and coaching, and for all the miles you put in week after week, if you're going to have a bad day in a race it will most likely be the run where it goes wrong. What makes this hard to accept is that we learn to run long before we start swimming or first ride a bike. Running is our most natural activity, and yet we often find ourselves hitting the wall hardest during the run phase of a race. Even more vexing is that this phenomenon seems to occur regardless of the race distance. Whether it's a sprint event or a full Iron-distance race, in the last mile or so of the run we struggle to remain strong.

The reason behind the phenomenon is obvious. Being the *last* phase of the race, the run is about more than just running. The cumulative fatigue of the previous miles and modalities makes our legs feel that much heavier, threatening to put us flat on the pavement with every step. Every race should be a great experience full of memories. Athletes form those experiences and memories into a story. As a form of expression, running is the climactic moment. A single turned ankle or cramp can mean the difference between a fairy tale ending and a Greek tragedy.

Every athlete has a story about how he found himself with an empty tank halfway through the race, ran on nothing except willpower, and gutted it out all the way to the finish. These are great stories, and hopefully we learn something from them as athletes; namely, that willpower and guts aren't the fastest way to get to the finish line. An athlete who continually relies on mental or intestinal fortitude might want to consider a different approach. There are two sides to every story, and the flip side of "I toughed it out all the way to the finish" could be "I overdid it all the way to T2."

The run is just the third act of the triathlete's story. Like any good drama, it depends on the previous sequence of events. If the hero is to emerge victorious, she needs to go begin her quest with all the necessary tools. With that said, every triathlete knows how to swim, how to bike, and how to run. But knowing how to do those three things doesn't necessarily mean you know how to race a triathlon. As a race, the triathlon is greater than the sum of its parts. The best athletes in the world focus on their technique in each discipline but manage their effort in the context of the entire race. Much of their understanding has been gained from professional coaching, years of experience, and through no small amount of trial and error. For age-group athletes who don't race as regularly and have limited time to actually train in a race environment, there's even more guesswork involved. It doesn't have to be that way. There has been a great deal of scientific research on holistic strategies for pacing in triathlons, and the information gained from it may unlock potential you never knew you had.

Let's take a look at your race story and see if we can rewrite the ending.

Note: As with everything else in this book, the data in this chapter comes from research published in peer-reviewed scientific journals. However, this data is unique because it deals with the performance of human beings rather than of materials and bicycles. In other words, there's more physiology than physics involved. No two human bodies are alike, and the studies cited typically observed the performance of small groups of athletes (20 or fewer) of varying degrees of athletic ability. Findings and conclusions deal in trends and indications. What we can learn from these studies strongly suggests specific pathways to success, but it is doubtful that we'll ever reach conclusive or definitive answers. Individual results can and will vary. What science shows us is a possible road to faster racing. Finding which specific lane works best for you on that road is a matter of experimentation and coaching according to your goals and resources.

DROPPING THE HAMMER: HOW TO FINISH FASTER ON SPRINT- & OLYMPIC-DISTANCE COURSES

There's an old saying among scuba divers: Slow is smooth and smooth is fast. In other words, it's best not to panic and try to rush yourself when dealing with an emergency situation while on a limited air supply deep under the water. You're more likely to make a mistake and turn a bad situation into a disastrous one. Triathletes should also take that lesson to heart because science gives us strong indications that we often find ourselves in similar circumstances on race day. We let nerves and adrenaline get the better of us, do things we typically wouldn't, and wind up in trouble. Pushing the pace while there's still too much distance between you and the finish line can feel a lot like drowning; you can't get enough air to the muscles, and a burning sensation of acid accumulating from anaerobic processes sets in until finally it overwhelms you and you have to be rescued.

This is the trend demonstrated by triathletes time and again. Regardless of your experience, ability level, or race distance, research indicates that an overwhelming majority of triathletes misjudge or abuse their most fundamental piece of racing equipment: their own bodies.

The effect of pacing during the swim was discussed previously in Chapter 2 (Fishtailing: The Benefit of Drafting Other Swimmers, page 31). The findings in the referenced study indicate that swimming at 80–85 percent of maximum effort allows a triathlete more power on the bike and more speed on the run, perhaps shaving as much as 1:45 off a sprint-distance triathlon.[1] Scientists concluded that higher efforts on the swim initiate anaerobic mechanisms that produce lactic acid and contribute to fatigue throughout the rest of the race. It might then be supposed that an athlete could maximize his race time by starting out of the first transition also at a submaximal pace and then building his effort throughout the rest of the race to a mad dash for the last mile or so of the run. The farther you get, the faster you can go because you have less to worry about lactate buildup, right?

Maybe not.

Another study put a group of age-group triathletes through a series of tests involving cycling for 20 minutes on a stationary bike with a device known as an ergometer that controls resistance to equalize power, followed by a 5-kilometer run. Each athlete performed the test four times, cycling (in random order) at 81–85 percent, 86–90 percent, 91–95 percent, and 96–100 percent of his maximum sustainable power. The study found that even though the triathletes ran progressively more slowly as they increased their effort on the bike, their overall time decreased.[2] *The indication is that for a sprint-distance event, the best strategy is to draft off the fastest swimmer you can at an 80–85 percent effort level, hammer the bike leg, and hang on for the run. No guts, no glory.*

But just because there are guts involved doesn't mean there's no room for brains. Two other studies indicate that the most crucial 2 miles for sprint- and Olympic-distance triathletes are those just before and just after the second transition. Researchers observed that it is the habit of many high-level triathletes to ease up in the last mile of the bike before transition in order to let their legs prepare for the run. However, traditional thinking suggests that you switch to a higher gear and increase your cadence before

T2. But that may not be the best approach. It's possible that ramping up your cycling cadence right before the run is detrimental to performance. One study again placed triathletes on a stationary bike for 20 minutes, followed by a 3-kilometer run. The other experiment ran longer, with a 65-minute bike leg and a 10-kilometer run.[3] Each study ran three iterations, ending the cycling leg with a slow, medium, and high cadence. They reached similar conclusions. To begin with, the researchers determined that cycling cadence had no significant effect on run performance, which is to say that the difference between results in each test condition was within a statistical margin of error. This goes back to the problem of indications versus conclusions. Running times *appeared* to be faster when athletes pedaled a slower cadence, but there weren't enough test subjects to establish a necessary degree of certainty.

Two out of three are good enough odds for most of us, but the scientific community prefers better odds, say ninety-nine out of a hundred. Such data exist, and they corroborate the finding that higher cycling cadence actually hurts you on the run. In a study that observed 107 professional athletes at the 2009 ETU European Triathlon Championships, the trend among athletes was to run each of the four laps of the course successively more slowly.[4] This may be related to one other effect noticed in the studies on pedaling cadence and running pace. Tests found that athletes who pedal at a higher cadence tend to run at a similar cadence in the first 500 meters after T2. It's possible that gearing down as you approach the transition may ramp your legs up to run faster than you actually want to, but this hasn't been studied enough to know for sure.

It's worth nothing that in both laboratory and race environments, triathletes express a remarkable trend that may explain why the all-or-nothing pacing strategy works best in short races.[5] In the 3-kilometer run test, the subjects began running at a fast pace, gradually slowed down over the course of the run until they hit the last 500 meters, and then gave a final burst to the finish. We see this phenomenon in races all the time, with the top leaders making the final push in an effort to mentally break their competitors and take the win. In this regard, the competitive spirit always defies science. We go beyond what the numbers say we should be able to do. But just because this strategy defies the numbers doesn't mean that it doesn't factor into the calculus of racing. Whether the run segment of a race is 3 kilometers or 13.1 miles, your last full measure is still only good for a few hundred meters. Those few hundred meters make up a significantly larger percentage of the total racecourse distance in a sprint event. Because of that, the initial and final bursts of speed coming out of transition and into the finish line have a greater impact on your overall performance and give less reason to worry about the performance dip in the middle segment of the run. From these trends, we can develop with reasonable assurance (but not certainty!) some basic guidelines for pacing strategy in sprint- and Olympic-distance races:

Pacing for Sprint-Distance Triathlons

- Swim at your 80–85 percent effort. Make every effort to draft another swimmer.

- Hammer the bike.

- Go out hard on the run, hang on until you hear the crowd cheering at the finish, and let the finish line fuel your last-gasp effort.

Pacing for Olympic-Distance Triathlons

- Swim at your 80–85 percent effort. Make every effort to draft another swimmer.

- Ride at a moderate cadence on the bike, below your lactate threshold.

– Run the first kilometer out of transition at a pace that is approximately 5 percent slower than what you want your overall speed to be, and then accelerate gradually all the way to the finish.[6]

Research indicates the underlying foundation for these strategic approaches. All studies demonstrate varying degrees of a trend with which we're familiar: The harder you go, the more quickly your body wears out. Although overall running speeds in the 3-kilometer and 5-kilometer distances were largely unaffected by cycling cadence, several metabolic factors are impacted. Trends suggest that heart rate and VO_2 decrease and blood lactate increases on the run as an athlete's cadence on the bike gets faster. This could explain why shifting and spinning going into T2 might cost you as you head out on the run. If you start the run at an overzealous pace, you'll be stuck with the resulting lactate doses all the way to the finish line. Again, these factors don't seem to make a great impact in a sprint event because lactate concentrations don't have enough time to create a substantial negative impact on performance and the competitive X factor is often strong enough to overcome it. But the longer you have to sustain the effort, the more you feel the burn, and the greater the problem compounds. *Metabolic factors, especially the buildup of lactate in the blood, become more important as the race distance increases.* Once you hit the 70.3- and 140.6-mile distances, race strategy becomes an entirely different affair involving a greater spectrum of unique variables.

Before getting into the research on pacing in a long-distance race, it helps to get some perspective on the race as a whole. Statistical research shows that every triathlete, regardless of ability level, spends about half of her race on the bike. The swim makes up about 10 percent and the run makes the other 40 percent of the triathlon. By the time you lace up your shoes and start the last 13.1 or 26.2 miles of a long race, you've already swum and biked either 57.2 or 114.4 miles. There's no avoiding the fact that the effort to get to T2 will have a significant cumulative effect on the body.

You won't be able to run as fast as you do on fresh legs. But no matter how easy you take it in the swim and on the bike, you still won't be completely fresh coming out of T2. It's not just about having enough energy to keep yourself from hitting the wall before the end, it's also about balancing your effort in all three events so that your speed in any one of them doesn't suffer unnecessarily. Success comes from optimizing performance across all three sports.

IT'S THE ECONOMY, STUPID: WHAT THE SMART ATHLETE KNOWS ABOUT PACING AN IRONMAN EFFORT

Everyone knows that racing at the 70.3- and 140.6-mile distances is a substantial physical undertaking for any human body. Many things happen to a triathlete's physiology as the mode of physical activity changes and the effort continues. There's no way for research to comprehensively study the effects of fitness, nutrition, anatomy, mind-set, gender, genetics, terrain, and weather conditions on a person's long-distance triathlon performance all at one time. For that reason, science's best efforts are limited to studies that isolate particular variables and examine their influence on triathletes while dismissing others that may or may not be equally important. Even with these limitations, research has developed some interesting data that can help triathletes make their own best efforts even better.

A study of 180 athletes who participated in Ironman Switzerland 2010 exhibited trends that give us a better picture of how triathletes typically approach race strategy. The athletes provided training data to the scientists for three months prior to the race. Their split and overall race times were recorded during the actual event.[7] The scientists found that triathletes went through the swim and bike legs at much higher speeds than those at which they trained. By contrast, their run speeds were much slower than in training.

The scientists took survey data from the race participants asking for their best finish times in both an Olympic-distance triathlon and a marathon. When they compared this data to their finish times in the Iron-distance race, they found a strong correlation. In fact, they developed an equation for predicting an Iron-distance race finish time based on Olympic-distance triathlon and marathon finish times:

Iron-Distance Finish Time (min.) = 152.1 + [1.332 × (Marathon PR)] + [1.964 × (Olympic-Distance PR)]

For the 126 participants in the study who had provided both a marathon and an Olympic-distance race time, the equation predicted a finish time of 684.9 minutes (+/- 74.2), and the average actual finish time was 691.1 minutes (+/- 83.3).[8] Given how close the estimated and actual results were for such a large group, the equation provides athletes with a way to make better use of early season training event times. Knowing within a certain range what your outcome ought to be gives you a better idea of how to set and achieve your goals. It bears noting here that the error in these results is over an hour, so you may want to use results from prior years to test how well this equation applies to you.

Having an accurate target for your overall finishing time is good, but actually achieving it is another matter. After all, what happened at Ironman Switzerland is hardly the exception; triathletes typically overdo it on the swim and the bike and then fade on the run. This is most likely correlated with the conclusions drawn from the studies on running in sprint- and Olympic-distance events, which indicate accumulated blood lactate becomes a serious problem late in the race. Drafting techniques on the swim portion of the race can save effort, and different technologies can ease the pain of maintaining speed on the bike. As we've already seen in Chapter 3, although many pieces of equipment can deliver a small advantage, a power meter will likely be a more valuable piece of racing equipment than any equally priced aerodynamic bike accessory. That should be even more evident now that we've seen that how you manage your engine on the bike can affect your speed not only in that leg of the triathlon, but also in the running miles that come afterward.

Studies on endurance athletes in competition indicate a tendency to adopt what is scientifically known as a positive pacing strategy. In this case, "positive" doesn't translate to "good," however. It refers to a race effort that starts out fast and slows down as the event progresses.[9] Researchers and athletes often share a problem when trying to detect positive pacing strategy. Most racecourses are either routed to be one large loop or an out-and-back over the same road. That makes it difficult to assess an athlete's effort level over the entire course because wind and terrain conditions constantly change in either scenario. Luckily, researchers found the consistency they needed for measuring positive pacing strategy during Ironman Western Australia in 2004. Before 2006, the bike course of that race consisted of three laps around the same road. Even better, the wind conditions allowed the researchers to define particular sections well enough to study the influence of headwinds and tailwinds on the triathletes. For their study, scientists installed power meters on the bikes of six male triathletes and measured their output over the course of the race.

Though there were only six test subjects, the results were surprisingly similar. To begin with, each triathlete's average power output went from 239 W to 203 W between the first and last lap and their average cadence dropped by 7 rpm. This decrease in output made for gradual increases in lap time, from an average of 97 minutes to complete the first lap to 101 minutes for the second to 108 to finish the third.[10] That's an average total of 306 minutes. With only an 11-minute difference between the first and third lap, using a power meter to balance out the overall effort would have saved 5 or 6 minutes at most (see What's It Worth?: The Relative Value of a Watt, page 55). That hardly seems worth the investment, but you need to look at the bigger picture. A set of good aero wheels might only save the same amount of time, and they would only help on the bike. The results of the Western Australia race study suggest a power meter would pay dividends long after T2.

That evidence comes from an analysis of how the triathletes produced power as the day wore on. Initially, they generated a strong amount of force on the pedals while turning them at a high velocity. In other words, they pushed hard in a big gear. But they wore down significantly on the second lap, spending more time either pedaling hard and slow or not so hard and slow. No feedback from the cyclists was taken, but we can reasonably figure out what happened using our own athletic experiences. Typically, we pedal hard and slow when accelerating or climbing, but the Western Australia course was about as flat as possible, with less than 40 feet of total elevation change.[11] So it's not a stretch to assume that during their second lap the cyclists fought to keep up the hard-and-fast effort, gradually failing to maintain the force in their legs, and then sputtered into a less-than-optimal effort before shifting out of their biggest gear. That assumption is reinforced by the evidence in their decreases in their hard-and-fast effort. It was cut nearly in half on each successive lap. The study focused exclusively on the bike phase, so no data on the competitors' run performance was published. However, all of the subjects finished within the top 10 percent, so it's reasonable to conclude they were well-trained and performed well on the marathon. The question remains how much better they could have done if they had taken better care of their legs on the bike.

The study cited two other findings that support the use of a power meter during a race. To begin with, even on a relatively flat course, the power output of the athletes fluctuated wildly throughout the day. This is common even among top professional athletes. No one's power profile during racing or training looks like a perfectly flat line, so the test subjects were not out of the ordinary. Changes in power output had no discernible relationship with changes in elevation or wind gusts on a moment-to-moment basis, leading the scientists to conclude they occurred at random. One thing was not as random in its impact, however, and that was wind direction. The power data showed a clear trend: a decrease in power output both when the athletes were riding into the wind as well as when they were riding *with* the wind. The indication is that they used the tailwind to take a breather rather than to pick up time, and that they were forced to reduce their effort anytime they encountered additional resistance. This is all characteristic of a triathlete who struggles late in the game. This is to say nothing of how fatigue influenced run performance.

Other studies indicate that better outcomes are possible when athletes understand the level to which they've trained and race within their performance limitations.[12] Although heart rate, speed, and cadence are good indicators of those limitations, changes in terrain and wind can make it difficult to accurately assess athletic performance. Measuring power is more accurate because it is a direct reflection of the effort your muscles apply to the pedals. Heart rate only measures cardiovascular performance, and recommended pedaling cadences are estimations based on what we know from power data. Ultimately, these are only indications and provide estimates for what we think we should be doing. By contrast, power is the exact thing we're trying to guess at with heart rate and cadence. For that reason, power is the best way to assess human performance on the bicycle. It directly measures our physiological output.

There are several books and web sites that detail methods for using power meters. A thorough explanation isn't intended for this work. However, with the material already covered in Chapter 3 you have a solid understanding of the fundamental principles. It doesn't require a great deal of reading to use a power meter beyond what you've already learned. In many ways, simply playing with a power meter will give you a much more valuable intuitive education because you will develop a feel for what certain effort levels on the computer feel like, and you'll correlate the two. Using it in the most basic way, a heart rate monitor tells you that you're pushing too hard before your body realizes it, and therefore helps you reel in an effort before it's unsalvageable. The same principle applies for a power meter. Even if you forgo the sophisticated training principles described in other books, a power meter can at least tell you when you're pedaling past the point of no return.

Based on the information researched throughout this book and the physical, logistical, and financial investments involved in competing in a long-distance triathlon, it's worth looking at race strategy recommendations from a holistic standpoint. This is not so much a summary as it is an application of the principles discussed throughout the work.

Pacing for Long-Distance Triathlons

- If your race is a 140.6-mile event, get in a good early-season marathon and Olympic-distance event as a gauge of what you might expect your overall Ironman course time to be.

- Know the course. Pay specific attention to wind speed and direction on the bike course, and to the location of any major hills on the run course.

- If you're ahead of the pack on the swim, you may be putting yourself behind the power curve. Regardless of ability, pushing past the 80–85 percent effort on the swim will most likely hurt your performance on the more important bike course.

- Drafting on the swim is typically a good idea (unless you get behind someone who's too slow).

- Use a power meter to pace your ride. A more informed athlete is a better athlete, and a better athlete always trumps a better bike.

- As long as you are moving faster than 15 mph on the bike, try to stay in the saddle on inclines. Aerodynamic resistance trumps road grade at high speeds. Standing up will create more surface area and resistance.

- Avoid gearing down and adopting a higher cadence during your last mile on the bike.

- Watch the hills on the run and try to maintain a sustainable effort rather than an even pace.

- Run the race as though it's 1 or 2 miles shorter than it actually is. Rely on the competitive instinct to give you the mental fuel to cross the line in the end. A faster pace throughout the entire course beats a 500-meter sprint to the end.

And there you have it. A complete, science-based approach to triathlon that hopefully gives you a few more tricks up your sleeve in your battle against the universe. We've seen what works, what works *better*, and perhaps most importantly, what doesn't work at all. Not that we've given you all the answers. There are still unsolved scientific mysteries in triathlon, and the next big leap in technology is always right around the corner. There are plenty of places you can look to keep up with developments, but you now have all the tools to understand the concepts behind emerging ideas and products. You don't have to look very far back through photos in triathlon history to see how wild ideas have cropped up over time. Beam bikes, elliptical chainrings, wet suit catch panels, and no end to unusual shoe designs have shown up in transition areas all over the world, and research has yet to fully validate or refute them. Still, no matter how new or radical an idea may seem, each relies on basic scientific principles. Armed with a comprehensive understanding of basic physics, you can objectively evaluate them for yourself with confidence.

Also keep in mind that as a science-minded triathlete, you are now engaged in a never-ending (and hopefully never boring!) process of experimentation and discovery. As we've said throughout this book, and several times in this chapter alone, there will always be outliers and variables we can't account for. You are a unique individual with a specific genetic code and an ability to set goals all your own. After you use what you've learned in this book to make any significant changes to your approach to training and racing, don't stop improving or tweaking! In a way, every triathlete is her own self-contained experiment. You hypothesize how much better you can be, and your race experience gives you a conclusion and analysis that allows you to refine your training. You'll no doubt want to come back and test new ideas to improve the outcome.

The triathlete's battle against the universe is never won. After each challenge is met, you're certain to find new environments and conditions against which to test yourself. What changes are the numbers and variables; the equations remain the same. With an equally solid application of your brain and body, I'm confident you'll see greater success in your racing.

NOTES

1: PHYSICS & THE TRIATHLETE

[1] Steven A. Brandt, Randall J. Stiles, John J. Bertin, and Ray Whitford, *Introduction to Aeronautics: A Design Perspective* (Reston, VA: American Institute of Aeronautics and Astronautics, 1997), 94.

[2] Ibid., 74.

[3] Angelo Armenti Jr., *The Physics of Sports* (New York: Springer-Verlag, 1996).

2: THE SWIM

[1] Steven A. Brandt, Randall J. Stiles, John J. Bertin, and Ray Whitford, *Introduction to Aeronautics: A Design Perspective* (Reston, VA: American Institute of Aeronautics and Astronautics, 1997), 53.

[2] Ibid., 15.

[3] Huub Toussaint, Maartje van Stralen, and Eric Stevens, "Wave Drag in Front Crawl Swimming" in *20 International Symposium on Biomechanics in Sports* (Amsterdam: Institute of Fundamental and Clinical Human Movement Science, Vrije Universiteit, 2002), 1.

[4] Official Records of the Olympic Movement, accessed May 18, 2013, http://www.olympic.org.

[5] Ibid.

[6] "2011 Dextro Energy Triathlon—ITU World Championship Grand Final Beijing Results," International Triathlon Union, accessed May 16, 2013, http://www.triathlon.org/results/results/2011_dextro_energy_triathlon_-_itu_world_championship_grand_final_beijing/6150/.

[7] "Ironman 70.3 Boulder Results," Ironman Live, accessed May 16, 2013, http://www.ironman.com/triathlon/events/ironman-70.3/boulder/results.aspx?y=2010#axzz2TWKpO1gg.

[8] "Ironman World Championship Official Results Guide 2011," World Triathlon Corporation, http://admin.ironman.com/assets/files/results/worldchampionship/2011.pdf.

[9] Toussaint et al., "Wave Drag in Front Crawl Swimming," 3.

[10] Daniel A. Marinho, Victor M. Reis, Francisco B. Alves, Leandro Machado, António J. Silva, and Abel I. Rouboa, "Hydrodynamic Drag During Gliding in Swimming," *Journal of Applied Biomechanics* 25, no. 3 (August 2009): 255.

[11] Ibid., 255.

[12] Huub Toussaint, "Strength Power and Technique of Swimming Performance: Science Meets Practice," *Wchwimmen Lernen und Optimieren* 1, no. 1 (2007): 7.

[13] Huub Toussaint, Anita Beelen, Anne Rodenburg, Anthony Sargeant, Gert de Groot, A. Peter Hollander, and Gerrit Jan van Ingen Schenau, "Propelling Efficiency of Front-Crawl Swimming" *Journal of Applied Physiology*, no. 68 (1988): 2510.

[14] Huub Toussaint and Peter J. Beek, "Biomechanics of Competitive Front Crawl Swimming," *Sports Medicine* 13, no. 1 (1992): 17.

[15] Mojmir Knapek, "Why Lift Is Unimportant in Swimming Propulsion," personal communication, May 27, 2001, http://www-rohan.sdsu.edu/dept/coachsci/swim/hydros/knapek.htm.

[16] Alberto E. Minetti, Georgios Machtsiras, and Jonathan C. Masters, "The Optimum Finger Spacing in Human Swimming," *Journal of Biomechanics* 42 (2009): 2188.

[17] Ibid., 2189.

[18] António José Silva, Abel Rouboa, António Moreira, Victor Machado Reis, Francisco Alves, João Paulo Vilas-Boas, and Daniel Almeida Marinho, "Analysis of Drafting Effects in Swimming Using Computational Fluid Dynamics," *Journal of Sports Science and Medicine* 7 (2008): 62.

[19] Jean-Claude Chatard and Barry Wilson, "Drafting Distance in Swimming," *Medicine and Science in Sports and Exercise* (2003): 1178.

[20] Peter Peeling and Grant Landers, "Swimming Intensity During Triathlon: A Review of Current Research and Strategies to Enhance Race Performance," *Journal of Sports Sciences* 27, no. 10 (August 2009): 1084.

[21] Chatard and Wilson, "Drafting Distance in Swimming," 1180.

[22] Brian Gettelfinger and E. L. Cussler, "Will Humans Swim Faster or Slower in Syrup?" *AIChE Journal* 50, no. 11 (2004): 2647.

[23] Joseph Kestin, Mordechai Sokolov, and William A. Wakeham, "Viscosity of Liquid Water in the Range -8°C to 150°C," *Journal of Physical Chemical Reference Data* 7, no. 3 (1978): 946.

[24] L. Cordain and R. Kopriva, "Wetsuits, Body Density and Swimming Performance," *Journal of Sports Medicine* 25, no. 1 (1991): 1.

[25] Huub Toussaint, Lex Bruinink, Remco Coster, Michiel de Looze, Bas Van Rossem, Ruurd Van Veenen, and Gert de Groot, "Effect of a Triathlon Wet Suit on Drag During Swimming," *Medicine and Science in Sports and Exercise* 21, no. 3 (1989): 321.

[26] J. C. Chatard, X. Senegas, M. Selles, P. Dreanot, and A. Geyssant, "Wet Suit Effect: A Comparison Between Competitive Swimmers and Triathletes," *Medicine and Science in Sports and Exercise* 27, no. 4 (April 1995): 584.

[27] A. Delextrat, T. Bernard, C. Hausswirth, F. Vercruyssen, and J. Brisswalter, "Effects of Swimming with a Wet Suit on Energy Expenditure During Subsequent Cycling," *Canadian Journal of Applied Physiology* 28, no. 3 (June 2003): 356.

[28] D. Perrier and K. M. Monteil, "Wetsuits and Performance: Influence of Technical Abilities," *Journal of Human Movement Studies* 41, no. 3 (2001).

[29] Huub Toussaint, Martin Truijens, Meint-Jan Elzinga, Ad van de van, Henk de Best, Bart Snabel, and Gert de Groot, "Effect of a Fast-skin 'Body' Suit on Drag During Front Crawl Swimming," *Sports Biomechanics* 1, no. 1 (January 2002): 8.

[30] Huub Toussaint, correspondence with the author, March 2012.

3: THE BIKE & POWER

[1] "Gerro's Milan-San Remo Power Analysis," accessed May 19, 2013, http://www
.cyclingtips.com.au/2012/03/gerros-milan-san-remo-power-analysis/.

[2] Whit Yost, "You Versus the Peloton," accessed May 19, 2013, http://www.bicycling
.com/news/2011-tour-de-france/tour-features/you-versus-peloton.

[3] Jeff Jones, "How Aero Is Aero?" accessed April 22, 2013, http://www.bikeradar
.com/gear/article/how-aero-is-aero-19273/; Allen Lim, "Introduction to Training with Power," accessed May 19, 2013, http://www.cycleops.com/cycleops
-university/athletes-cu.html.

4: THE BIKE: WEIGHT & AERODYNAMICS

[1] All data taken from Google Earth.

[2] Guy Kesteven, "Trek Equinox 7 Review," accessed January 8, 2011, http://www
.bikeradar.com/gear/category/bikes/time-trial-triathlon/product/review-trek
-equinox-7-09-32739.

[3] Mat Brett, "Trek Equinox TTX 9.0 Review," accessed January 8, 2011, http://www
.bikeradar.com/gear/category/bikes/time-trial-triathlon/product/review-trek
-equinox-ttx-90-09-32738.

[4] Data published by Bontrager, accessed April 30, 2012, http://bontrager.com.

[5] Data published by SRAM, accessed April 30, 2012, http://www.sram.com.

[6] Ibid.

[7] Raymond Britt, "Ironman Arizona: 3 Lap Bike Times and Speeds by Age Group,"
accessed March 9, 2012, http://www.runtri.com/2010/11/ironman-arizona-3
-lap-bike-times-and.html.

[8] Raymond Britt, "Ironman Wisconsin: Racing Advice, Analysis, Photos and More,"
accessed March 9, 2012, http://www.runtri.com/2007/07/ironman-wisconsin
-2007-what-to-expect.html.

[9] Records of the International Human Powered Vehicle Association, accessed April 20,
2012, http://www.ihpva.org/hpvarec3.htm#nom21.

[10] Vincent Chabroux, Caroline Barelle, and Daniel Favier, "Aerodynamics of Time Trial Bicycle Helmets," *Engineering of Sport 7*, no. 2 (2008): 405.

[11] Ibid.

[12] Jay Prasuhn, "Round Versus Aero: Aero Bikes Are in Fashion, but Are They Really Faster? *LAVA* Finds Out," *LAVA* 11 (April 2012): 19.

[13] Paul Harder, Doug Cusack, Carl Matson, and Mike Lavery, *Airfoil Development for the Trek Speed Concept Triathlon Bicycle* (Waterloo, WI: Trek Bicycle Corporation, 2010), 12.

[14] Stephanie Sidelko, "Benchmark of Aerodynamic Cycling Helmets Using a Refined Wind Tunnel Test Protocol for Helmet Drag Research" (thesis, Massachusetts Institute of Technology, 2007), 17.

[15] Ibid.

[16] Ibid.

[17] Records of the International Human Powered Vehicle Association, accessed February 4, 2012, http://www.ihpva.org/hpvarec3.htm#nom21.

[18] Ibid.

[19] Ibid.

[20] Len Brownlie, Peter Ostafichuk, Erik Tews, Hil Muller, Eamon Briggs, and Kevin Franks, "The Wind-Averaged Aerodynamic Drag of Competitive Time Trial Cycling Helmets" in *8th Conference of the International Sports Engineering Association* (Sheffield, UK: International Sports Engineering Association, 2010), 2422.

[21] Matthew N. Godo, David Corson, and Steve M. Legensk, *A Comparative Aerodynamic Study of Commercial Bicycle Wheels Using CFD* (Reston, VA: American Institute of Aeronautics and Astronautics, 2010), 8.

[22] Data published by Weather Underground, http://www.wunderground.com.

[23] Brownlie et al.,"The Wind-Averaged Aerodynamic Drag of Competitive Time Trial Cycling Helmets," *Procedia Engineering* 2 (2010): 2420.

[24] Chabroux, Barelle, and Favier, "Aerodynamics," 408.

[25] Ibid.

[26] Brownlie et al., "Wind-Averaged Aerodynamic Drag," 2420.

[27] Godo, Corson, and Legensk, *Comparative Aerodynamic Study*, 12.

[28] David Gordon Wilson, *Bicycling Science*, 3rd ed. (Cambridge, MA: MIT Press, 2004), 217.

[29] Kraig Willett and Al Morrison, "Roller Data," accessed January 3, 2012, http://biketechreview.com/tires/rolling-resistance/475-roller-data.

[30] Wilson, *Bicycling Science*, 226.

[31] Wilson, *Bicycling Science*, 227.

5: THE RUN

[1] Jinger S. Gottschall and Rodger Kram, "Ground Reaction Forces During Downhill and Uphill Running," *Journal of Biomechanics* 38, no. 3 (March 2005): 445.

[2] Ibid., 445.

[3] Ibid., 447.

[4] Andy Ruina, John E. A. Bertram, and Manoj Srinivasan, "A Collisional Model of the Energetic Cost of Support Work Qualitatively Explains Leg Sequencing in Walking and Galloping, Pseudo-Elastic Leg Behavior in Running and the Walk-to-Run Transition," *Journal of Theoretical Biology* 237, no. 2 (November 2005): 170.

[5] Claire T. Farley and Octavio Gonzalez, "Leg Stiffness and Stride Frequency in Human Running," *Journal of Biomechanics* 29, no. 2 (February 1996): 181.

[6] Bryan Heiderscheit, Elizabeth S. Chumanov, Max P. Michalski, Christa M. Wille, and Michael B. Ryan, "Effects of Step Rate Manipulation on Joint Mechanics During Running," *Medicine and Science in Sports and Exercise* 43, no. 2 (2011): 296.

[7] Darren J. Dutto and Gerald A. Smith, "Changes in Spring-Mass Characteristics During Treadmill Running to Exhaustion," *Medicine and Science in Sports & Exercise* 34, no. 8 (August 2002): 324; Giuseppe Rabita, Jean Slawinski, Olivier Girard, Frank Bignet, and Christophe Hausswirth, "Spring-Mass Behavior During Exhaustive Run at Constant Velocity in Elite Triathletes," *Medicine & Science in Sports and Exercise* 43, no. 4 (April 2011): 685.

[8] Rabita et al., "Spring-Mass Behavior," 685.

[9] R. Margaria, P. Cerretelli, P. Aghemo, and G. Sassi, "Energy Cost of Running," *Journal of Applied Physiology* 18, no. 2 (1963): 368.

[10] Michael Fowler, "Galileo: Scaling," lesson slides, University of Virginia Physics Department, accessed April 10, 2013, http://galileo.phys.virginia.edu/classes/609 .ral5q.fall04/LecturePDF/L14-GALILEOSCALING.pdf.

[11] Daniel E. Lieberman and Dennis M. Bramble, "The Evolution of Marathon Running: Capabilities in Humans," *Journal of Sports Medicine* 37 (2007): 289.

[12] Jim Reardon, "The Physics of Running," presentation, University of Wisconsin Chaos and Complex Systems Seminar, 2005.

[13] Ibid.

[14] B. C. Elliott and B. A. Blanksby, "Optimal Stride Length Considerations for Male and Female Recreational Runners," *British Journal of Sports Medicine* 13, no. 1 (April 1979): 16.

[15] Jim Reardon, correspondence with the author, April 25, 2012.

[16] Richard J. de Dear, Edward Arens, Zhang Hui, and Masayuki Oguro, "Convective and Radiative Heat Transfer Coefficients for Individual Human Body Segments," *International Journal of Biometeorology* 40, no. 3 (May 1997): 141.

[17] Steven C. Dennis and Timothy D. Noakes, "Advantages of a Smaller Bodymass in Humans When Distance-Running in Warm, Humid Conditions," *European Journal of Applied Physiology* 79, no. 3 (February 1999): 361.

[18] Ibid., 361.

[19] Frank E. Marino, Ziphelele Mbambo, Edith Kortekaas, Gary Wilson, Mike I. Lambert, Timothy D. Noakes, and Steven C. Dennis, "Advantages of Smaller Body Mass During Distance Running in Warm, Humid Environments," *European Journal of Physiology* 441 (December 2000): 281.

[20] L. Brownlie, I. Mekjavic, I. Gartshore, B. Mutch, and E. Banister, "The Influence of Apparel on Aerodynamic Drag in Running," *Annual of Physiological Anthropology* 6, no. 3 (July 1987): 133.

[21] Tim Noakes, *Lore of Running* (Cape Town: Oxford University Press, 1985), 59.

[22] Brownlie et al., "Influence of Apparel," 133.

[23] Ibid., 138.

[24] Ibid.

[25] C. T. M. Davies, "Effects of Wind Assistance and Resistance on the Forward Motion of a Runner," *Journal of Applied Physiology* 48 (1980): 708.

[26] Philip E. Martin, "Mechanical and Physiological Responses to Lower Extremity Loading During Running," *Medicine and Science in Sports and Exercise* 17, no. 4 (August 1985): 427.

[27] Data from Newton Running.

[28] Data from Nike.

[29] Data from Zoot Sports.

[30] Data from Adidas, accessed April 10, 2013, http://www.adidas.com.

[31] Data from KSwiss, accessed April 10, 2013, http://www.kswiss.com.

[32] Martin, "Mechanical and Physiological Responses," 429.

[33] Noakes, *Lore of Running*, 57.

[34] Lin Wang, Youlian Hong, and Jing Xian Li, "Durability of Running Shoes with Ethylene Vinyl Acetate or Polyurethane Midsoles," *Journal of Sports Sciences* 30, no. 16 (2012): 1789.

[35] Ibid.

[36] R. Clinghan, G. P. Arnold, T. S. Drew, L. A. Cochrane, and R. J. Abboud, "Do You Get Value for Money When You Buy an Expensive Pair of Running Shoes?" *British Journal of Sports Medicine* 42, no. 3 (2008): 93.

[37] Peter J. McNair and Robert N. Marshall, "Kinematic and Kinetic Parameters Associated with Running in Different Shoes," *British Journal of Sports Medicine* 28, no. 4 (1994): 260.

[38] R. D. Thomson, A. E. Birkbeck, W. T. Tan, L. F. McCafferty, S. Grant, and J. Wilson, "The Modelling and Performance of Training Shoe Cushioning Systems," *Sports Engineering* 2 (1999): 119.

[39] Wang, Hong, and Li, "Durability of Running Shoes," 1791.

[40] Jih-Lei Liang and Hung-Ta Chiu, "Cushioning of the Running Shoes After Long-Term Use," Proceedings of the International Symposium on Biomechanics in Sports 28 (2010), 3–4; Wang, Hong, and Li, "Durability of Running Shoes," 1792; P. W. Kong, N. G. Candelaria, and D. R. Smith, "Running in New and Worn Shoes: A Comparison of Three Types of Footwear," *British Journal of Sports Medicine* 43, no. 10 (2009): 748.

41 Gina Kolata, "When to Retire a Running Shoe," *The New York Times Online*, accessed February 18, 2013, http://well.blogs.nytimes.com/2013/02/18/when-to-retire -a-running-shoe.

42 Kong, Candelaria, and Smith, "New and Worn Shoes," 748.

43 H. C. Pinnington and B. Dawson, "Running Economy of Elite Surf Iron Men and Male Runners, on Soft Dry Beach Sand and Grass," *European Journal of Applied Physiology* 86, no. 1 (November 2001): 65.

44 Aldo Sassi, Alessandro Stefanescu, Paolo Menaspa, Andrea Bosio, Marco Riggio, and Ermanno Rampinini, "The Cost of Running on Natural Grass and Artificial Turf Surfaces," *Journal of Strength and Conditioning Research* 25, no. 3 (March 2011): 606.

45 Data from Zoot Sports.

46 Andrew M. Jones and Jonathan H. Doust, "A 1% Treadmill Grade Most Accurately Reflects the Energetic Cost of Outdoor Running," *Journal of Sports Sciences* 14, no. 4 (August 1996): 321.

6: A SCIENTIFIC APPROACH TO RACING STRATEGY

1 Jean-Claude Chatard and Barry Wilson, "Drafting Distance in Swimming," *Medicine and Science in Sports and Exercise* (2003): 1180.

2 Robert Suriano and David Bishop, "Combined Cycle and Run Performance Is Maximised When the Cycle Is Completed at the Highest Sustainable Intensity," *European Journal of Applied Physiology* 11, no. 4 (November 2010): 753.

3 T. Bernard, F. Vercruyssen, F. Grego, C. Hausswirth, R. Lepers, J-M Vallier, and J. Brisswalter, "Effect of Cycling Cadence on Subsequent 3 km Running Performance in Well Trained Triathletes," *British Journal of Sports Medicine* 37, no. 2 (April 2003): 154; Gary A. Tew, "The Effect of Cycling Cadence on Subsequent 10km Running Performance in Well-Trained Triathletes," *Journal of Sports Science and Medicine* 4 (February 2005): 342.

4 Yann Le Meur, Thierry Bernard, Sylvian Dorel, Chriss Abbiss, Gerard, Honnorat, Jean-ick Brisswalter, and Christophe Hausswirth, "Relationships Between Triathlon Performance and Pacing Strategy During the Run in an International Competition," *International Journal of Sports Physiology and Performance* 6, no. 2 (June 2011): 183.

[5] Olivier Hue, Daniel Le Gallais, Didier Chollet, Alain Boussana, and Christian Prefaut, "The Influence of Prior Cycling on Biomechanical and Cardiorespiratory Response Profiles During Running in Triathletes," *European Journal of Applied Physiology 77* (1998): 103.

[6] Christophe Hausswirth, Yann Le Meur, Francois Bieuzen, Jeanick Brisswalter, and Thierry Bernard, "Pacing Strategy During the Initial Phase of the Run in Triathlon: Influence on Overall Performance," *European Journal of Applied Physiology* 108, no. 6 (April 2010): 1115.

[7] Chrisoph Alexander Rust, Beat Knechtle, Patrizia Knechtle, Thomas Rosemann, and Rouald Lepers, "Personal Best Times in an Olympic Distance Triathlon and in a Marathon Predict Ironman Race Time in Recreational Male Triathletes," *Open Access Journal of Sports Medicine* 2 (August 2011): 122.

[8] Ibid., 124.

[9] Chris R. Abbiss, Marc J. Quod, David T. Martin, Kevin Netto, Kazunori Nosaka, Hamilton Lee, Rob Suriano, David Bishop, and Paul B. Laursen, "Dynamic Pacing Strategies During the Cycle Phase of an Ironman Triathlon," *Medicine and Science in Sports and Exercise* 38, no. 4 (April 2006): 726.

[10] Ibid., 729.

[11] Abbiss et al., "Dynamic Pacing Strategies," 729.

[12] Foster et al., "Effect of Pacing Strategy on Cycle Time Trial Performance," 387; C. O. Mattern, R. W. Kenefick, R. Kertzer, and T. J. Quinn, "Impact of Starting Strategy on Cycling Performance," *International Journal of Sports Medicine* 22, no. 5 (July 2001): 353.

GLOSSARY

Acceleration. The rate of change of a body's velocity. Positive acceleration indicates the body is increasing its velocity in the desired direction. Negative acceleration indicates a decrease in velocity.

Aerodynamic resistance. Also referred to as *drag* or *drag force*. Aerodynamic resistance is a force that opposes a body's motion as a result of the body's movement through air. There are many forms of aerodynamic drag based upon the size, shape, and velocity of the body, as well as the relative density, velocity, and direction of the air's movement.

Aerodynamics. The study of the flow of air. It is a specialized field in the broader subject of fluid dynamics, which includes the behavior of other gases and liquids.

Airfoil. A shape of specific geometry typically associated with the cross section of a wing. It is described both by its aerodynamic properties in generating lift and drag, as well as a particular set of geometric measurements defining its shape. The airfoil shape is the foundation of most aerodynamic designs in cycling and triathlon.

Angle of attack. The lengthwise orientation of an object with regard to its direction of travel. A high angle of attack is typically associated with greater lift and drag.

Apparent wind. The wind as it is experienced from the perspective of a moving object. Both the direction and the velocity of the apparent wind depend on the motion of the object because the object's motion influences its frame of reference.

Bernoulli's principle. An aerodynamic principle discovered by Italian scientist Daniel Bernoulli in 1738. It states, among other things, that the pressure of a fluid is directly related to the velocity of its flow. An increase in a fluid field's flow velocity will result in a decrease in pressure.

Body. An object held in consideration as pertaining to how it interacts with a designated medium. It could be either a subatomic particle or a planet. In classical physics, it is typically a physical object defined by its properties of mass and kinetic energy.

Buoyancy. An object's characteristic ability to float on top of a particular fluid. Buoyancy is dependent upon an object's mass and volume, as well as the density of the fluid. As the object sinks into a fluid, it will displace a volume of water equal to the volume of the portion that is submerged. When the weight of the displaced fluid is equal to the weight of the object, it will not sink farther.

Clincher tires. In cycling, tires that are separate from their inner tubes. Also referred to as *open tubular*.

Coefficient of friction. A dimensionless number that describes the amount of friction between two objects in contact with each other. It depends on several variables, including the chemical and physical properties of the two surfaces, as well as the amount of force between them. Because the coefficient of friction cannot be calculated, it is always derived from standardized experimental measurements.

Coefficient of rolling resistance. A dimensionless number that describes the interaction between a rolling body such as a wheel and a surface. It is much like the coefficient of friction, except that it is measured as an object rolls rather than slides across a surface.

Contact patch. The area of a tire's surface that is in contact with the ground. It is based on road surface conditions and the material properties of the tire and its air pressure.

Convection. The transfer of heat through a fluid medium. In the case of athletics, this usually means air or water. Convection occurs as a result of air or water flowing over the surface of the skin. Heat energy is exchanged from the warmer surface to the cooler medium. Convection is not related to the evaporation of sweat (perspiration).

Deformation. A change in a solid body's shape, usually as a result of some force acting upon it.

Density. The concentration of mass within an object, defined as the ratio of its mass to volume.

Displacement. The space within a fluid medium occupied by an object as it is immersed in the fluid. The volume of the immersed portion of the body is equal to the volume of displaced fluid, and can be used to calculate the body's buoyancy in that fluid.

Drafting. The act of following closely behind an object in order to minimize aerodynamic resistance.

Drag. See aerodynamic resistance.

Drag coefficient (C_d). A dimensionless number used to characterize a body's interaction with a fluid medium as a result of its movement. Because it cannot be calculated, the drag coefficient is obtained through standardized measurements and is generally accepted as consistent for most geometric body shapes, to include airfoils, in a specified range of atmospheric conditions.

Effective crosswind. The direction and magnitude of aerodynamic resistance calculated after accounting for the wind direction and velocity in relation to that of the body in consideration. By adding the headwind and crosswind components together, the effective crosswind vector shows the aerodynamic force experienced by the body.

Evaporation. The change of state from liquid to gas as a result of heat energy causing a fluid's molecules to become excited.

Force. In physics, an influence that causes a change in a body's position or energy state.

Friction. The molecular interaction between two objects as they move while in contact with each other. It is measured as a force and is defined mathematically as the product of the normal force and the coefficient of friction.

Frontal area. The portion of a body's surface area that is directly exposed to contact with a fluid medium.

Grade. The measurement of a hill's incline as a percentage. It is found by dividing the increase in elevation over a given distance, multiplied by 100. A hill's grade generally changes constantly, but is averaged over the total distance of the ascent.

Gravitational force. The amount of force exerted on a body as a consequence of the gravitational force and that body's total mass.

Gravity. The tendency of all physical objects to attract each other as a consequence of their mass. The gravitational force between two objects depends on their respective masses and the distance between them. Because the earth is sufficiently larger than all other objects on it, the acceleration of gravity is held as a constant value of 9.81 m/s^2.

Hysteresis. In bicycle tires, the changing of the tire's shape as a consequence of its interaction with the contact surface. These changes of shape create elastic deformation and vibration. Both processes require energy from the system. Because the only producer of energy is the cyclist, tire designers attempt to limit hysteresis as much as possible.

Impact. The force experienced in the short time span when two objects collide.

Induced drag. The drag created by an object as a consequence of its angle of attack relative to the wind. As the angle of attack increases, more surface area on the underside of the object is exposed to airflow. This typically increases lift, but also contributes to greater drag as well.

Kilogram-force. A standard of metric measurement of force, defined as the amount of force exerted by a mass of one kilogram in a gravitational field of 9.81 m/s², also known as "earth standard gravity." The kilogram-force is the basis of conversion between pounds and kilograms, and is also the foundation of measurement of aerodynamic drag in bicycle design.

Lift. An aerodynamic force that acts on a body in a direction perpendicular to its drag.

Mass. The measure of the amount of matter in an object.

Medium. The physical environment through which a body moves. It possesses certain physical characteristics that define how it exerts influence on the body as a result of its motion.

Newton's laws. Three laws of motion of an object outlined by Sir Isaac Newton in his 1687 book *Philosophiae Naturalis Principia Mathematica*. They contribute to the foundation of classical mechanics. In brief, they are as follows:

> **First Law:** An object at rest will remain so unless acted upon by a force. An object in motion will continue to do so unless also acted upon by a force.

> **Second Law:** A body's acceleration is directly proportionate to its mass and the sum of the forces acting upon it.

Newton's laws, continued

Third Law: When a force is exerted on a body, the body will exert an equal force in the opposite direction.

Normal force. The force exerted by a solid surface on a body resting upon it. Typically, the normal force is equal to the force of gravity the object experiences.

Open tubular tires. In cycling, tires with an integrated tube. Also often referred to as *sew ups*.

Power. A physical measurement of the amount of work performed during a specified period of time. Power can be expressed in many forms. Typical mathematical units defining it are horsepower and watts.

Pressure drag. Also known as form drag, it is the drag that results directly from the size and shape of a body moving through a fluid medium, and is proportionate to the square of its velocity. Bodies with higher frontal area or longer cross section will experience greater pressure drag than other bodies at the same velocity.

Propulsion, or thrust. A force that causes a body to move in its desired direction.

Radiation. The emission of heat energy as a form of electromagnetic waves. All objects radiate heat energy. In athletic competition, radiation makes the smallest contribution to heat transfer.

Reynolds number. A dimensionless number that characterizes how a fluid field will interact with a body moving through it as a result of the body's size and the velocity of the flow field.

Rolling resistance. The force acting against a wheel's motion as a result of its interaction with the surface. Rolling resistance is a product of the normal force (or the total weight acting on the wheel) and the coefficient of friction. The power required to overcome rolling resistance is directly proportionate to the bike's velocity.

Scaling. The study of certain principles of physics as they pertain to how the size of a physical object influences its properties, most often associated with but not limited to biological organisms. The study of scaling has helped to understand several aspects of human physiological performance.

Skin friction drag. The drag experienced by a body moving through a fluid as a direct result of the fluid's frictional interaction with the body's surface. At low speeds such as those experienced in cycling and running, skin friction drag has negligible influence on performance. It is more significant in swimming.

Terminal Velocity. The velocity of a body at which the aerodynamic forces opposing its motion equal the gravitational force pulling it downward. Because aerodynamic resistance is a function of velocity, nearly all objects will reach a sufficient speed such that aerodynamic forces equal gravitational forces. Because the sum of the forces equals zero, there will be no acceleration and velocity will no longer increase, thus the qualification as terminal.

Traction. Frictional force as it applies to holding a body against a surface, usually considered a "helpful" form of friction that assists rather than resists forward motion.

Tubular tires. In cycling, tires with an integrated inner tube. Also referred to as *sew ups*.

Turbulence. A region of unsteady, chaotic flow in a fluid field, often caused by an object passing through it.

Velocity. The rate of a body's change in position as a function of time. Often referred to as its speed.

Viscosity. A measure of a fluid's resistance to flow.

VO₂max. A measure of a biological organism's aerobic capacity, typically measured in units of ml/kg/min, or milliliters of oxygen consumed per 1 kilogram of body mass per minute of time. It can be used to estimate the organism's maximum aerobic effort or its relative endurance.

Volume. The measure of space occupied by an object. It is the product of an object's length, width, and height, and can therefore be measured in cubic units, such as meters-cubed. There are also equivalent standards of fluid-based measurement, such as liters.

Vortex. In aerodynamics, a localized area of extreme low pressure that disturbs the flow of air molecules and can generate a force opposing a solid body's progress in its direction of motion.

Watt. A measurement of power, named after Scottish inventor and engineer James Watt. One watt is expressed as 1 joule per second.

Wave drag. Drag created by pressurized waves ahead of a body moving through a fluid medium. The creation of these waves requires a significant amount of energy, which is taken from that generated by the swimmer.

Weight. The force exerted by gravity on a body. It can be calculated either in newtons or pounds.

Wind tunnel. A device used to measure the aerodynamic properties of an object. It consists of a system that can generate a uniform airflow through an enclosed tunnel, a test stand upon which the object of investigation is placed, and instrumentation to measure various aerodynamic interactions.

Yaw angle. The angle of difference between the wind direction and a body's direction of travel.

INDEX

A

Acceleration
    in force equation, 6, 20, 52
    in free fall, 75
    in water, 26
Action and reaction, 7
Aerodynamics, 78–98
    airfoil, forces acting on, 21–22
    bike equipment and, 47, 82–85
        crosswinds and, 96–98
        helmets, 87, 88, 89, 92–93
        wind tunnel tests, 84, 88–89,
            91, 102–106
    body position of cyclist and, 82–83
    crosswinds, 93–98
    drag, 9–14, 85–91
    frontal area influence on, 2, 3, 82
    importance of, 78
    overview of, 9–14
    power requirements influenced by,
        79–83
    power to overcome forces of, 90–91
    resistance increase with speed,
        79–80
    in running, 141–143
    terminal velocity and, 76–77
    terminology of, 86
Airfoil
    forces acting on, 21–22
    power savings associated with
        shape, 81–82
Air resistance. *See also* Aerodynamics
    crosswinds, 93–98
    power needed to maintain speed
        with increasing, 79, 80
    speed and, 79–82
    terminal velocity and, 76–77
Aluminum vs. carbon fiber bikes,
    69–70
Angle of attack, induced drag and, 12
Angle of incline
    calculating force acting against
        cyclist, 64–65

Physics and the triathlete, 1–15
    aerodynamics, 9–14
    force, 4–7
    friction, 8–9
Plateau, breaking through, 115
Pogo stick, running analogous to, 122,
    125
Power
    in cycling, 45–46, 52–58
        aerodynamics and, 79–83,
            90–92
        to maintain speed uphill,
            65–66
        to maintain speed with increas-
            ing air resistance, 79, 80
        to overcome rolling resistance,
            110–112
        position of cyclist and, 82–83,
            90
        weight influence on, 66–67
    defined, 49
    equation for, 55
    importance of measuring, 51
    in long-distance triathlons,
        165–166
    time saved with power savings, 92
    velocity related to, 79–81
    wattage, 49, 55–58
Power meter, 48–51, 65, 163–167
Power-to-weight ratio, 72
Power zones, 57
Pressure drag
    in cycling, 45
    described, 10–11
    in water, 22–25, 34, 36
Propulsion
    in cycling, 45–46
    in running, 117–122, 127
    in water, 25–29, 31
Propulsive efficiency, 26, 27

R

Race number, 114
Radiation, thermal, 138
Reynolds number, 36
Rims. *See* Wheels
Road grade
    affect on running pace, 144–145
    corresponding angle of incline, 63
    gravitational force and, 61–65
Rolling resistance, 44, 60–61, 108–112
Running, 115–153
    aerodynamics in, 141–143
    apparel, 147
    drafting, 141–143
    efficiency
        cadence and, 126–127, 134–135
        of different species, 131–133
        increasing, methods for, 123–127
        size effects on, 128–135
        stride length and, 123, 125–127,
            134–135
        vertical displacement and,
            123–127, 133–134
    heat dissipation vs. athlete size,
        135–141
    on hills, 143–145
    mechanics of, 117–122
        breaking force, 118, 121–122
        friction and, 121–122
        impact force, 118, 120, 123, 131,
            149, 150, 152
        pendulum motion, 122–123
        phases on motion, 118–119
        pogo stick analogy, 122, 125
        tuning up, 122–128
        vertical and horizontal force
            components, 120–122, 123
    on natural surfaces, 151–152
    pace strategy, 158–162
    shoes, 146–151
    on treadmills, 152–153

Running economy. *See also* Running, efficiency
    influence of surface type on, 152
    mechanics of, 122–128
    success of Kenyan runners and, 128–135

S

Scaling, 130, 133, 135
Sculling, 29
Second law of motion, Newton's, 6, 52, 74
Shape. *See also* Aerodynamics
    airfoil, 21–22, 81–82
    drag coefficient and, 14
Shaved legs, 114
Shoes, running, 146–151
    cushioning and energy return, 147–150
    sole, 147–151
    weight, 146–147
Size
    heat dissipation vs. athlete size, 135–141
    running efficiency and, 128–135
Skin area, 135. *See also* Surface area
Skin friction drag
    in cycling, 45
    described, 11–12
    swimsuit design and, 39
    in water, 24–25, 34, 36, 39
Skin suit, cycling, 114
Speed
    air resistance effects on, 79–82
    cycling uphill, 65
    heat production as function of, 135–137, 139–140
    impact of weight loss on, 66–67
    influence on apparent wind, 97–98
    power to overcome rolling resistance and, 110–112

power-velocity relationship, 79–81
Speedo (Fastskin swimsuit), 38, 39
SRM Power Meter blog, 50
Strategy, 155–169
    for long-distance triathlons, 162–168
    for Olympic-distance triathlons, 160–161
    power meter use, 163–167
    for sprint-distance triathlons, 160
Strava, 50
Stride length, running efficiency and, 123, 125–127, 134–135
Stride rate, running efficiency and, 126–127, 134–135
Surface area
    changing, 2–3
    frontal area, 2, 3, 11–14, 82
    as function of mass, 135, 136
    of hands moving in water, 31
    heat dissipation and, 137–141
    as physical property of body, 2
Swimming, 17–40. *See also* wet suit/swim skin, 36–40
    buoyancy and lift, 19–22
    drafting, 31–33
    drag, 22–25
    forces on body in water, 18–29
    hand shape, 29–31
    importance of technique, 27, 38
    kicking technique, 27–29
    pace, 33, 158–162
    physiological performance during, 27
    propulsion (thrust), 25–29
    weight and, 19
Swim skin, 36–40

T

Terminal velocity, 76–77
Thermal radiation, 138

ABOUT THE AUTHOR

JIM GOURLEY is a successful triathlete, four-time Ironman finisher, and part of a four-man-division team that
finished the Race Across America, one of the most difficult endurance
races in the world. Gourley earned a degree in astronautical engineering
from the United States Air Force Academy and has written on the scientific and technological developments in sports for the last four years. His
articles have appeared in *Triathlete, Inside Triathlon, LAVA, 220 Triathlon*,
and *3/GO* magazines, as well as in *Peloton* and *Bicycle Times*. This is his
first book.